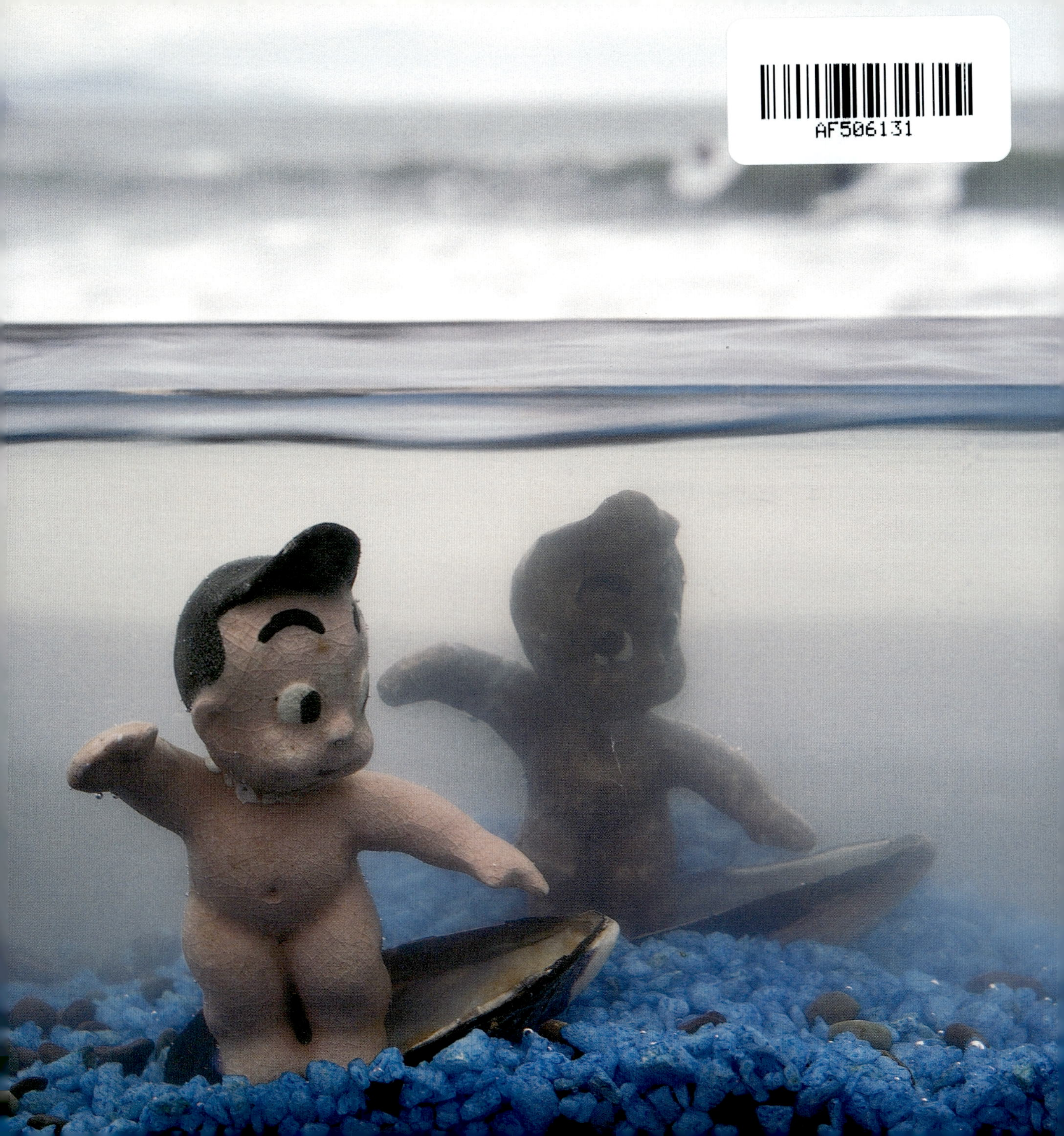
AF506131

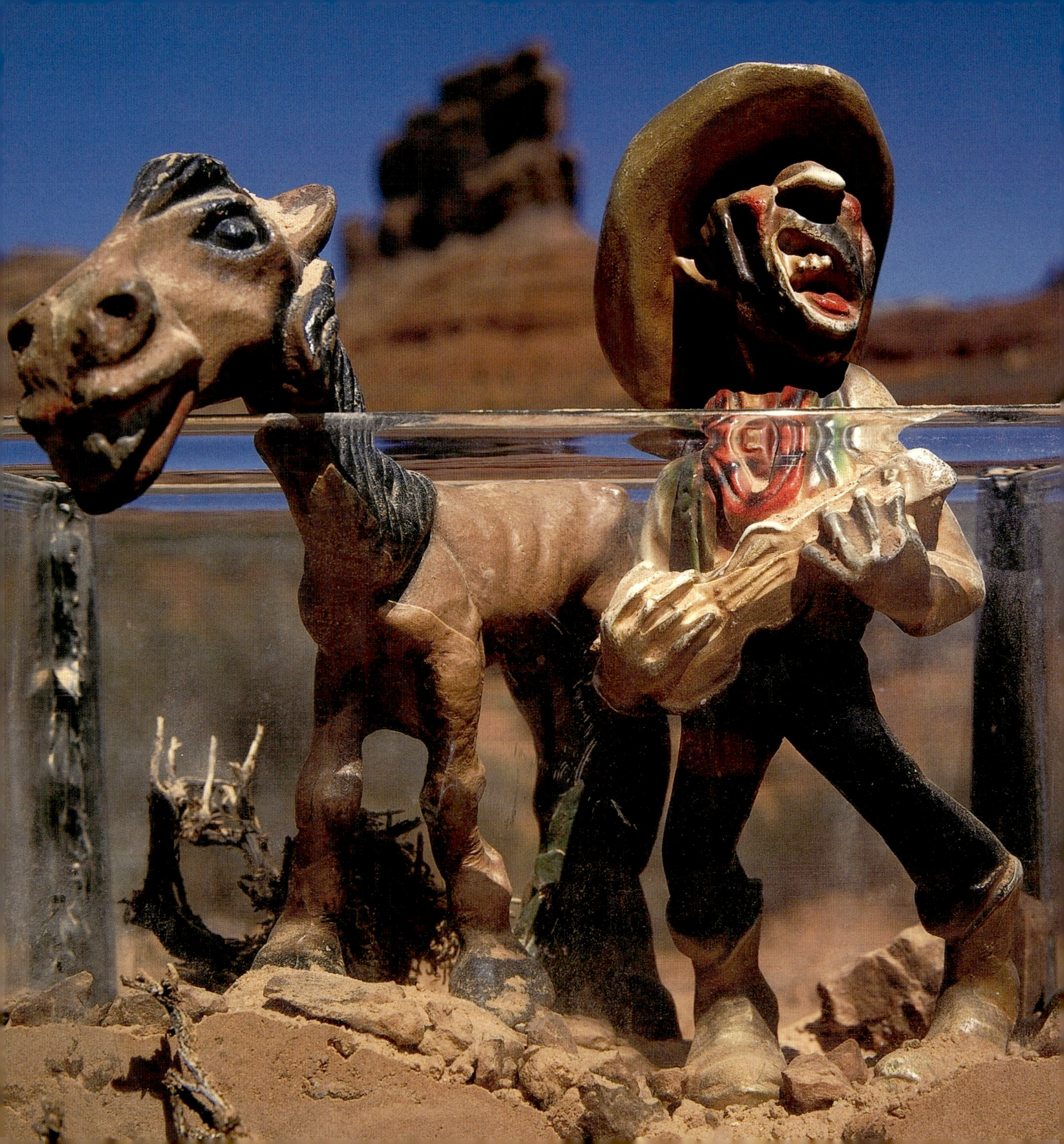

Arthur Tress
Fish Tank Sonata

A Bulfinch Press Book
Little, Brown and Company
Boston / New York / London

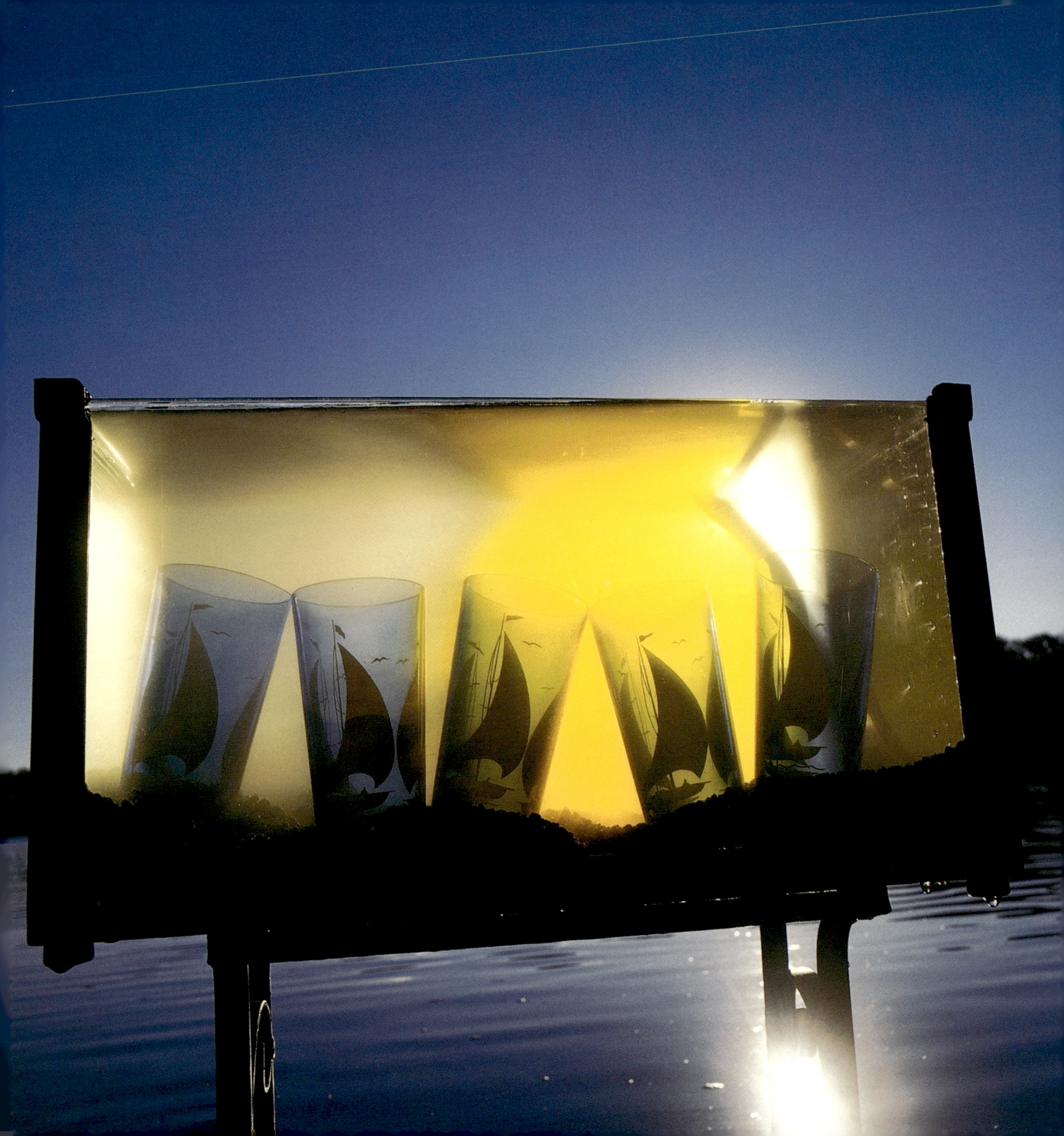

I.
On the Water

The first of five movements, in which a fisherman enters the river. He dreams about his catch, but waits for hours. Then a spirit fish jumps into his boat and volunteers to be his guide to the secrets of successful angling, as demonstrated by the instinctive hunting techniques of nature and professional competition. The fish has other secrets to divulge as well.

When the fisherman slipped his boat
Into lazy currents along the bank,
He watched his line until it sank
In bright water, rippling and mute.
And as the day lifted, shimmered, and turned,
He knew that something wonderful might be learned.

2]

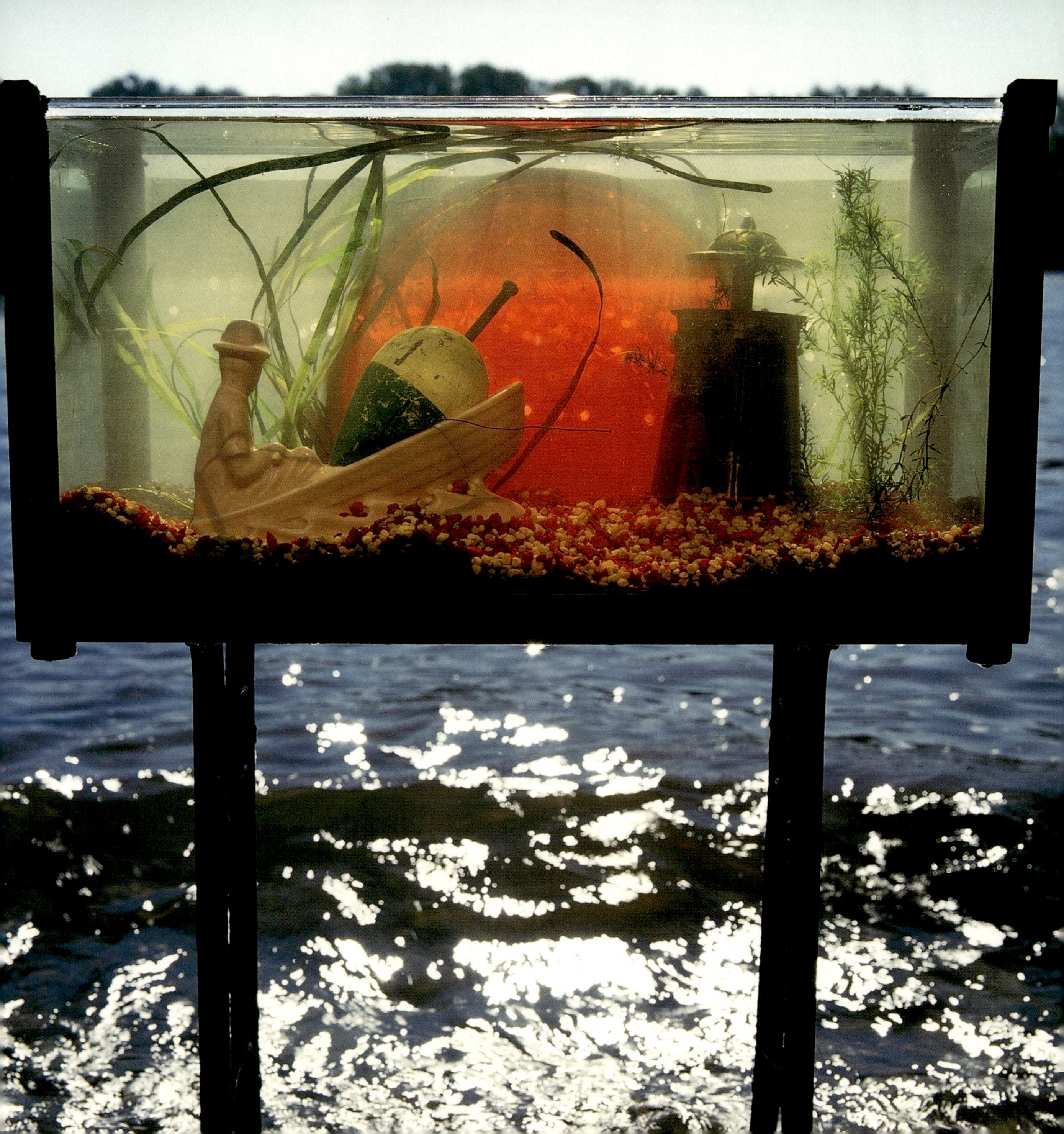

As he drifted he dreamed about
His creel filled with struggling trout.
Of succulent meals
And luscious aromas,
Golden brown skin
And the flesh therein.

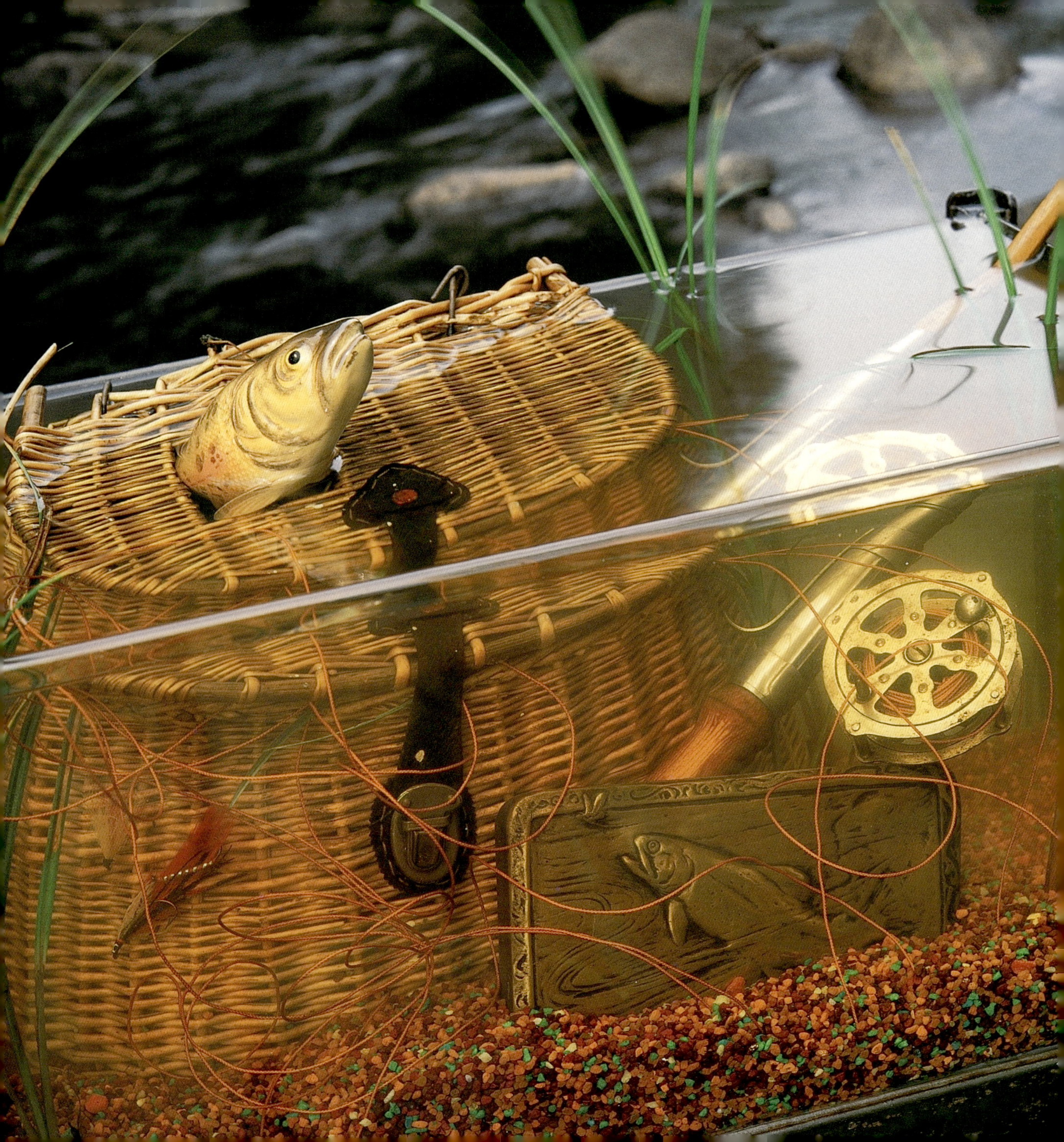

To memorialize his wiggling prizes
He'd photograph each and keep them,

So at a glance his every guest
Could ponder the nature
Of the angler's quest.

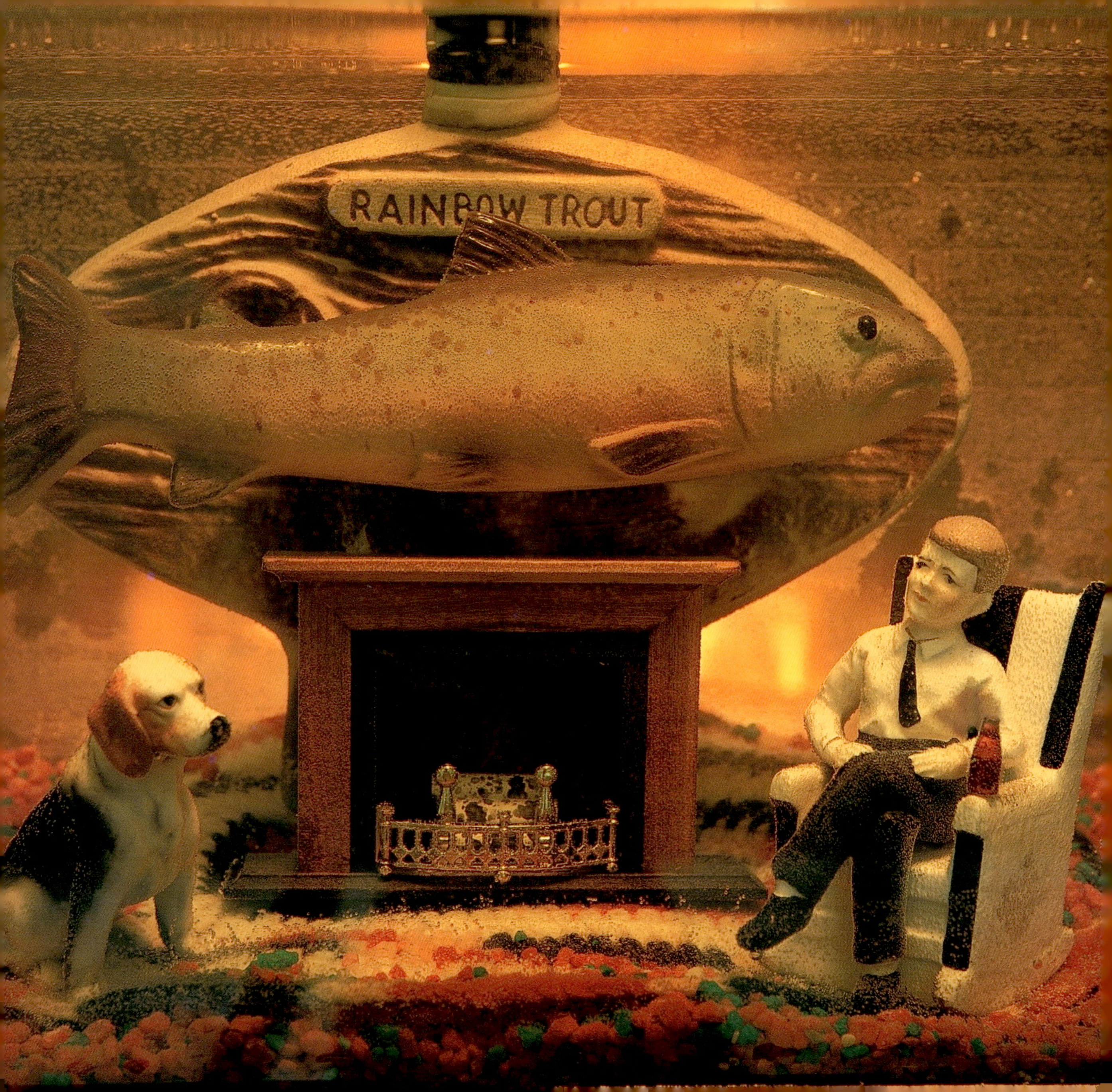

RAINBOW TROUT

And any who'd listen would have no doubt
Of the manly deeds he's talked about.

He'd be elected someday
By the old barroom crowd
To the Happy Angler's Club
Trolling the clouds.

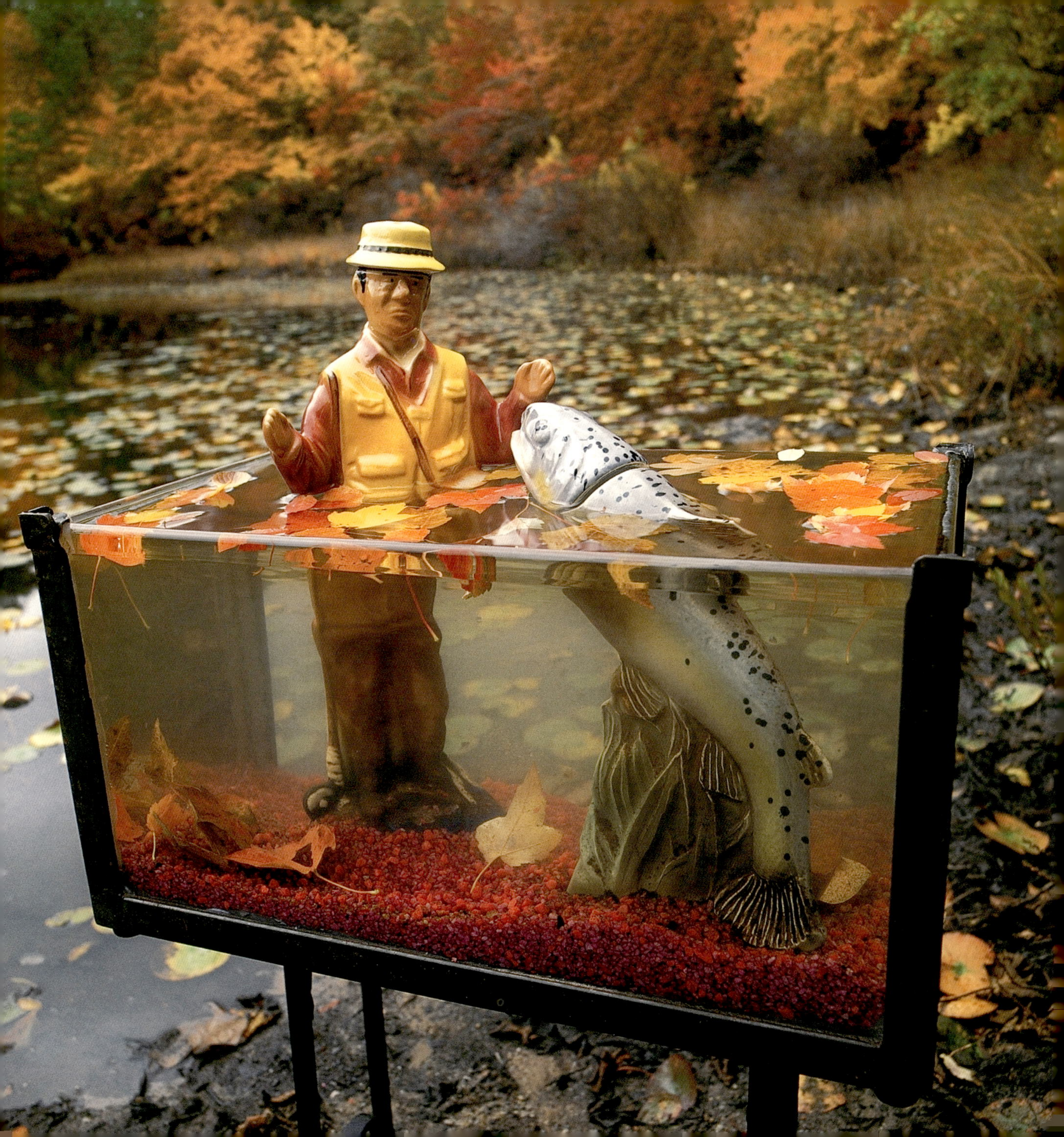

Lilies wavered upon the limpid stream,
Absorbing the sun in a flowery dream.
A crane serenely hidden
Among the weeds
Burst into flight
To wake him from his reveries.

10

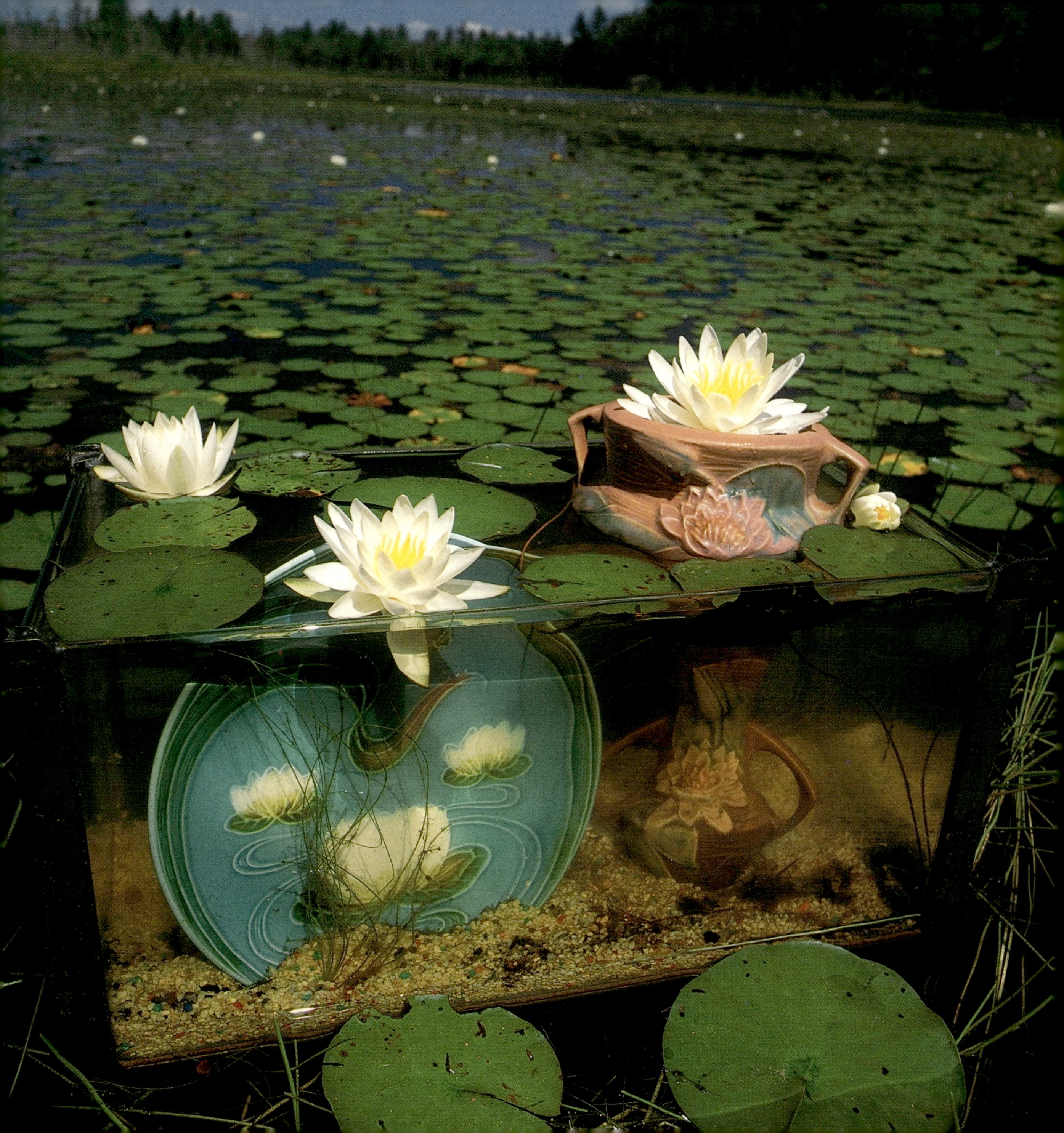

The patient heron plucked minnows galore
From the aquatic pasture below the rower's oars.

But the man felt
Not a nibble on his line;
He cursed the elusive fish
For being so malign.

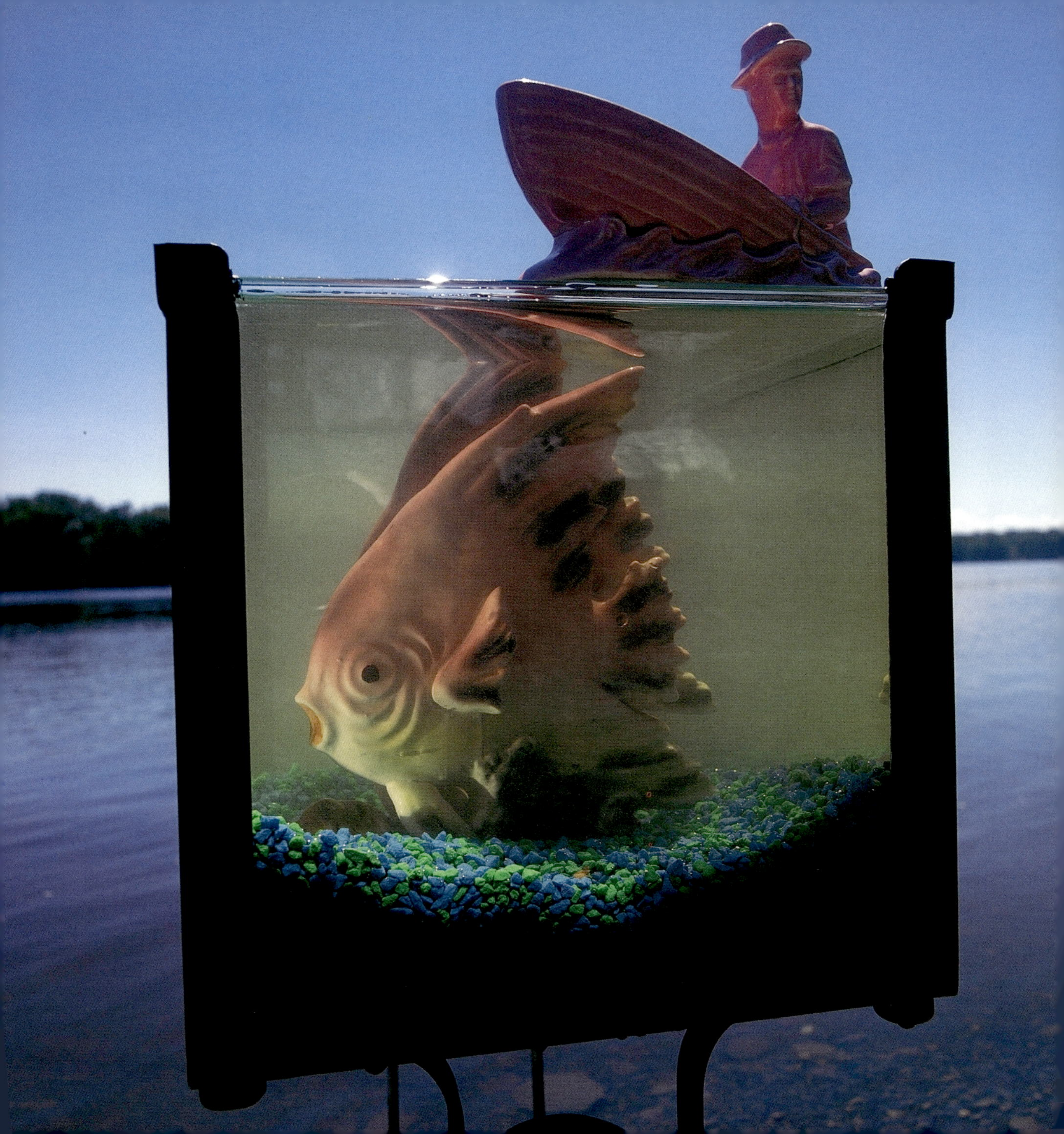

A strange occurrence then befell him.
From the water rose a red snapper
Who fell into his boat and began to tell him,

Listen closely to me;
I'll tell you what I can—
All the lore and secrets
Of fishing unknown to man.
I'll be your eternal key
To know the water's vast fecundity.

14)

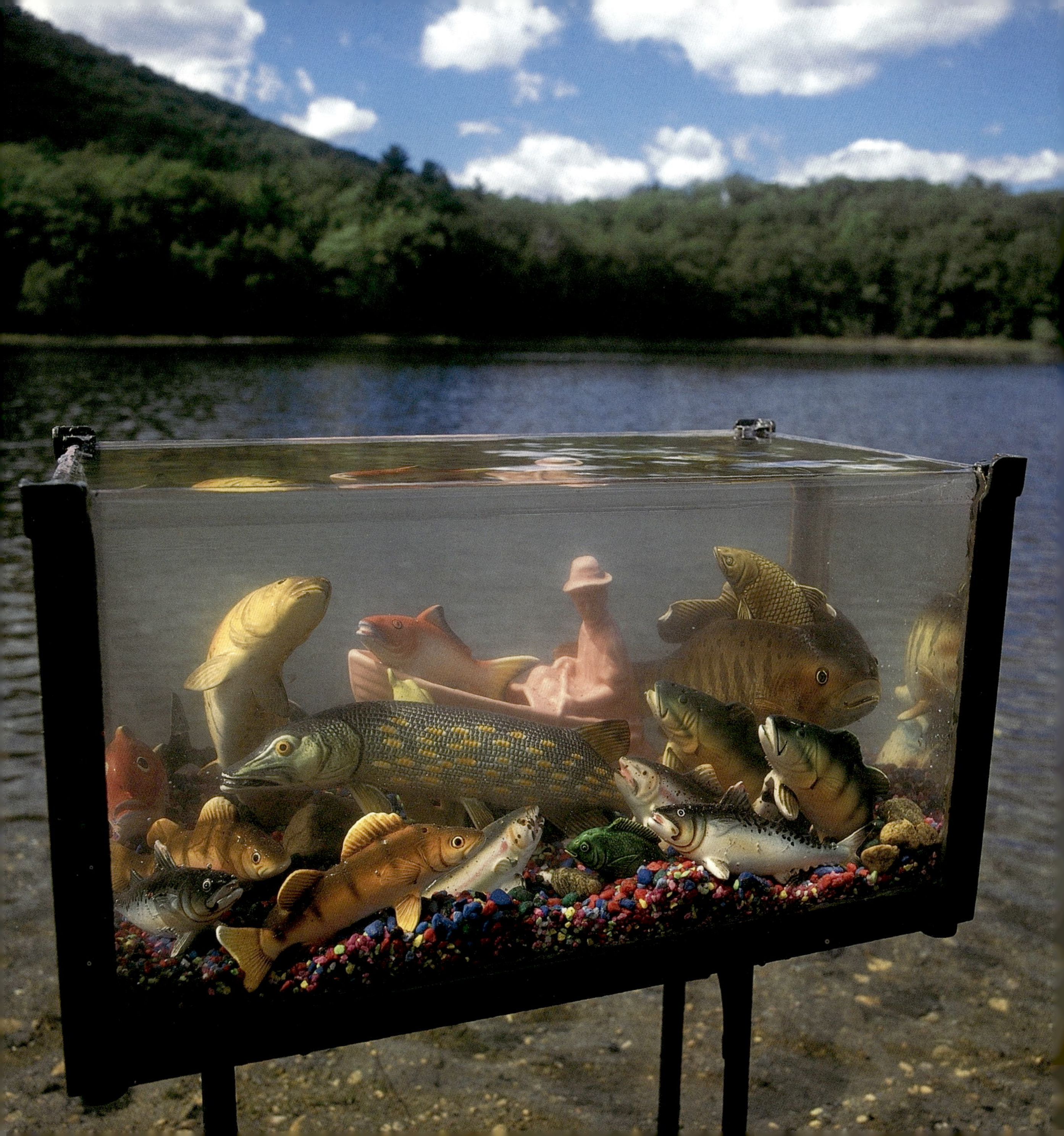

First, anatomy: bones and spines,
fins and scales; dorsal to the ventral—
Unique and perfect body lines
To speed the fish and hide him.

Yet measure by more than length alone.
The fish is part of his aquatic home—
Reeds and mud, shadows and deeps,
All inseparable from the fish that leaps.

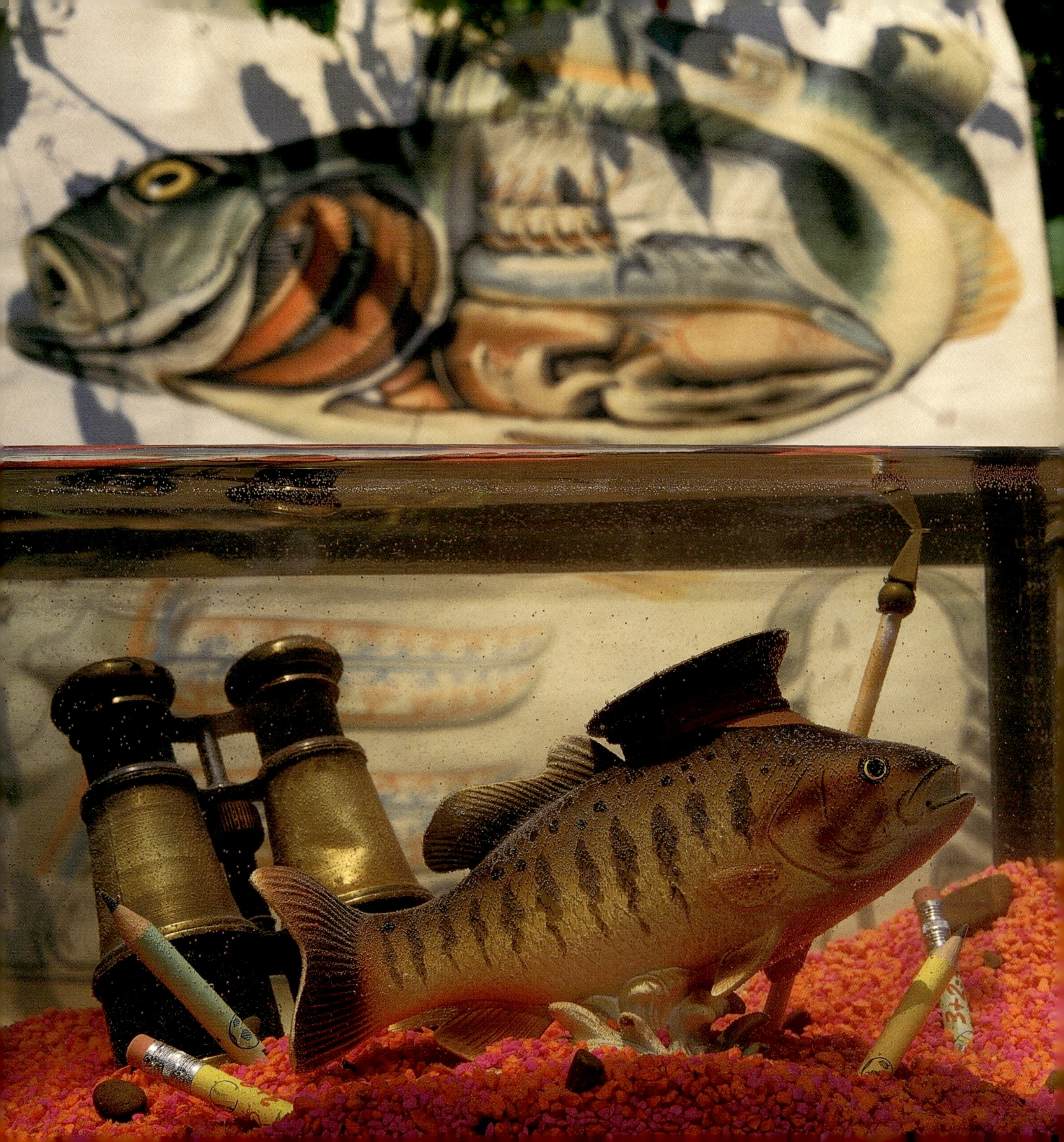

You must learn to know
Where the trout will teem
In the swirls and eddies
Of the mountain stream.

By rising plumes
Of dark river murk
In deep-running channels
You'll see where they lurk.

18]

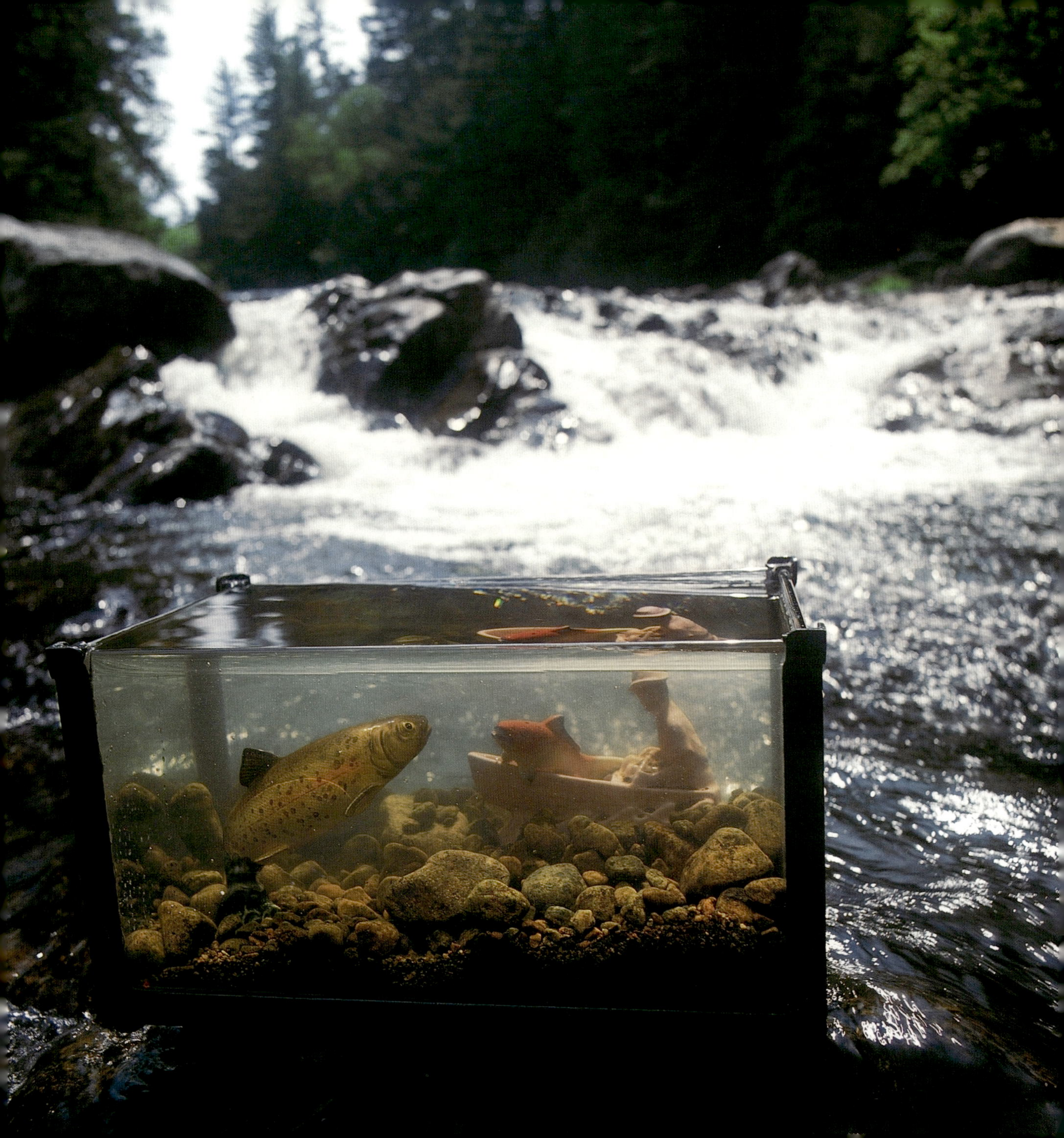

As on the firing range you gain the skills
To hit the target through endless drills.

But in an open field one day
All that practice will fall away,
Leaving only you to contemplate
The direction that your aim must take.

20)

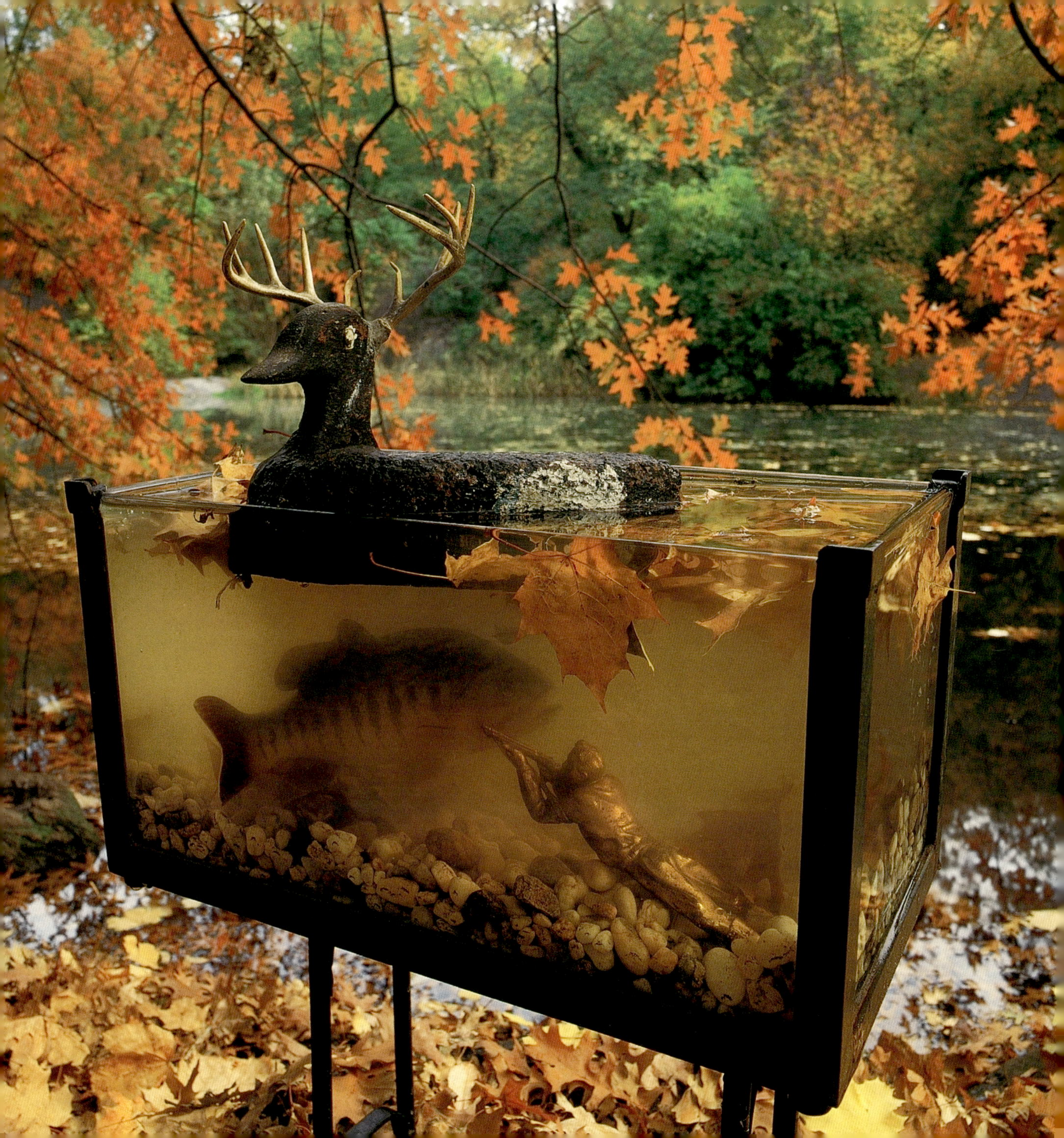

Be like the sharp-eyed Indian
Who reads the ripples on the river's flow
Before he thrusts his spear below.

Know the casual abandon
Of the bear, and his poise—
He swats up the fish
Like his own little toys.

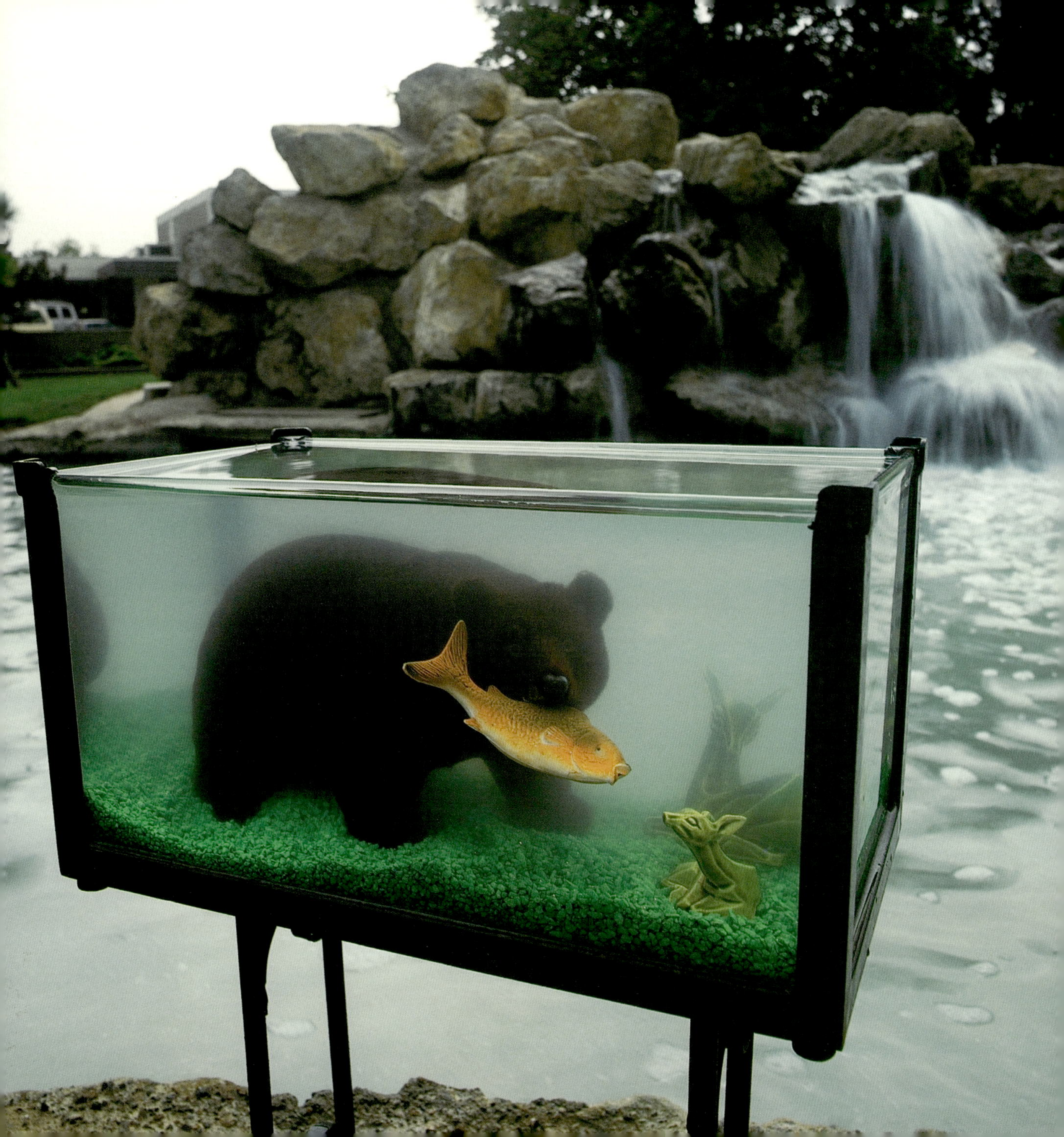

Like the long-distance swimmer
You must steel your will
Against endless labors
And bone-gnawing chill.

24]

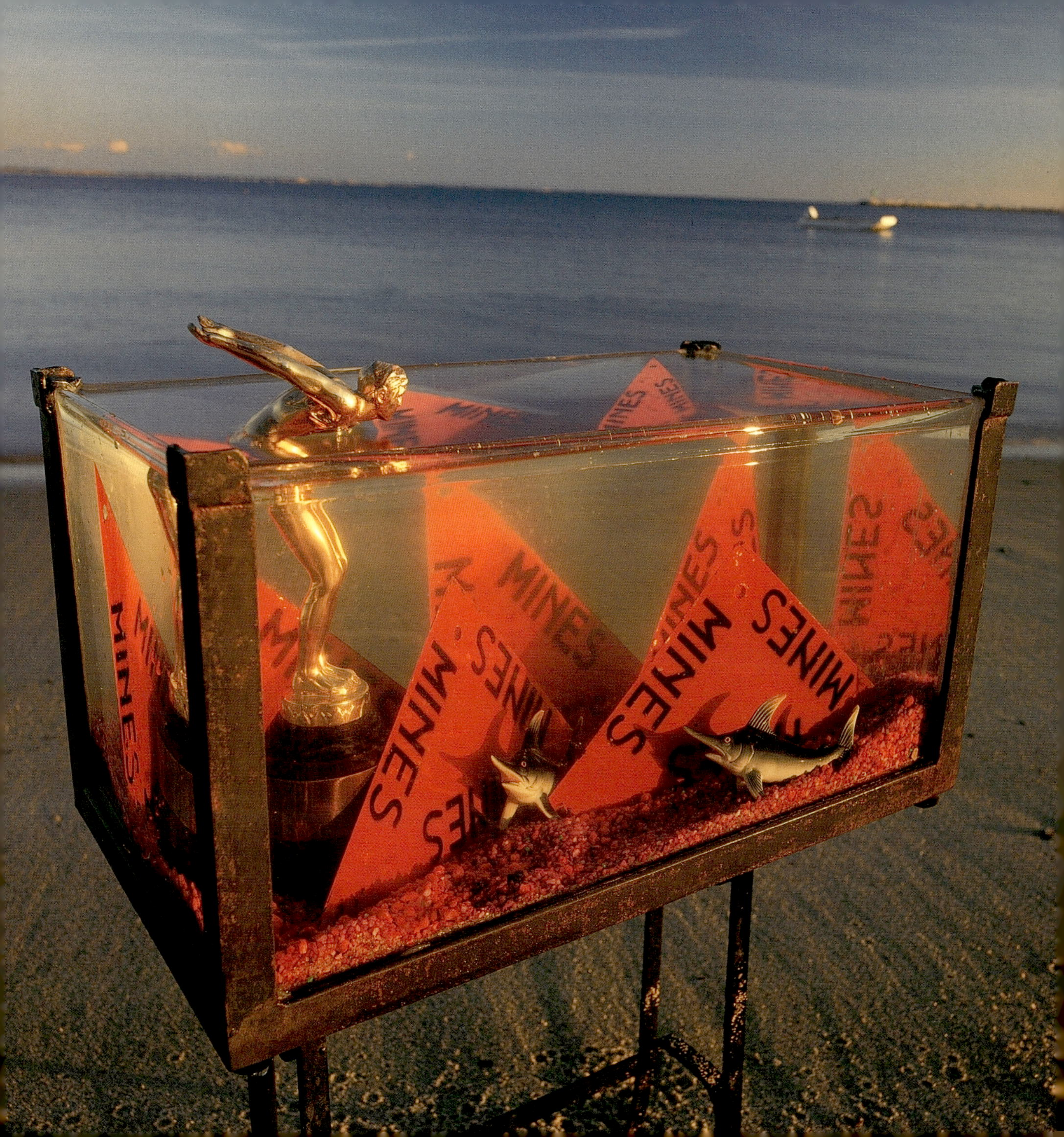
MINES
MINES
MINES
MINES
MINES
MINES
MINES
MINES
MINES

And emulate the championship golfer
Who once his stroke's begun
Tunes out the pressing crowd
To get the hole in one.

26]

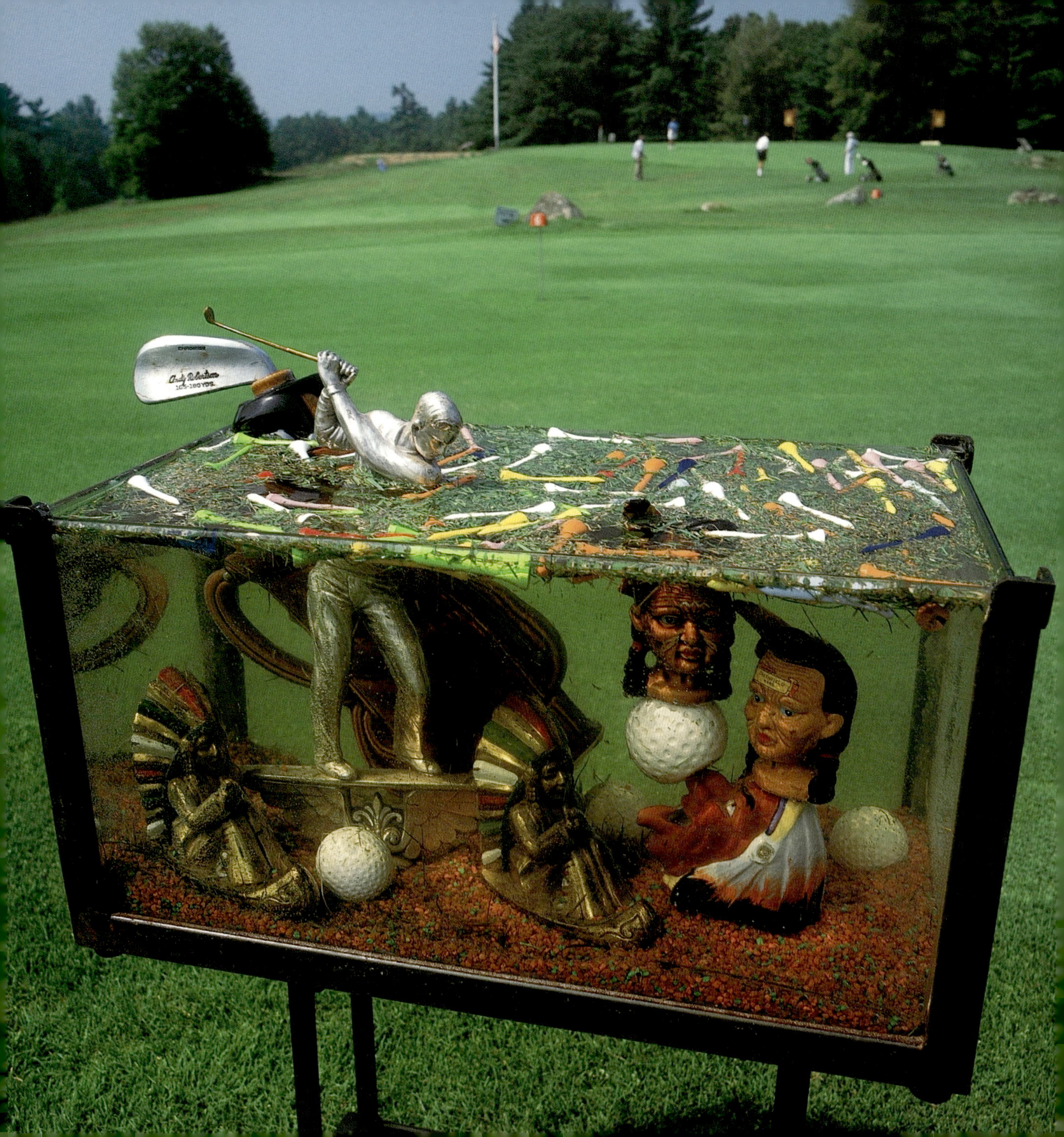

The volleyball captain
Lands endless aces
By anticipating his opponent's
Brief unguarded places.

28)

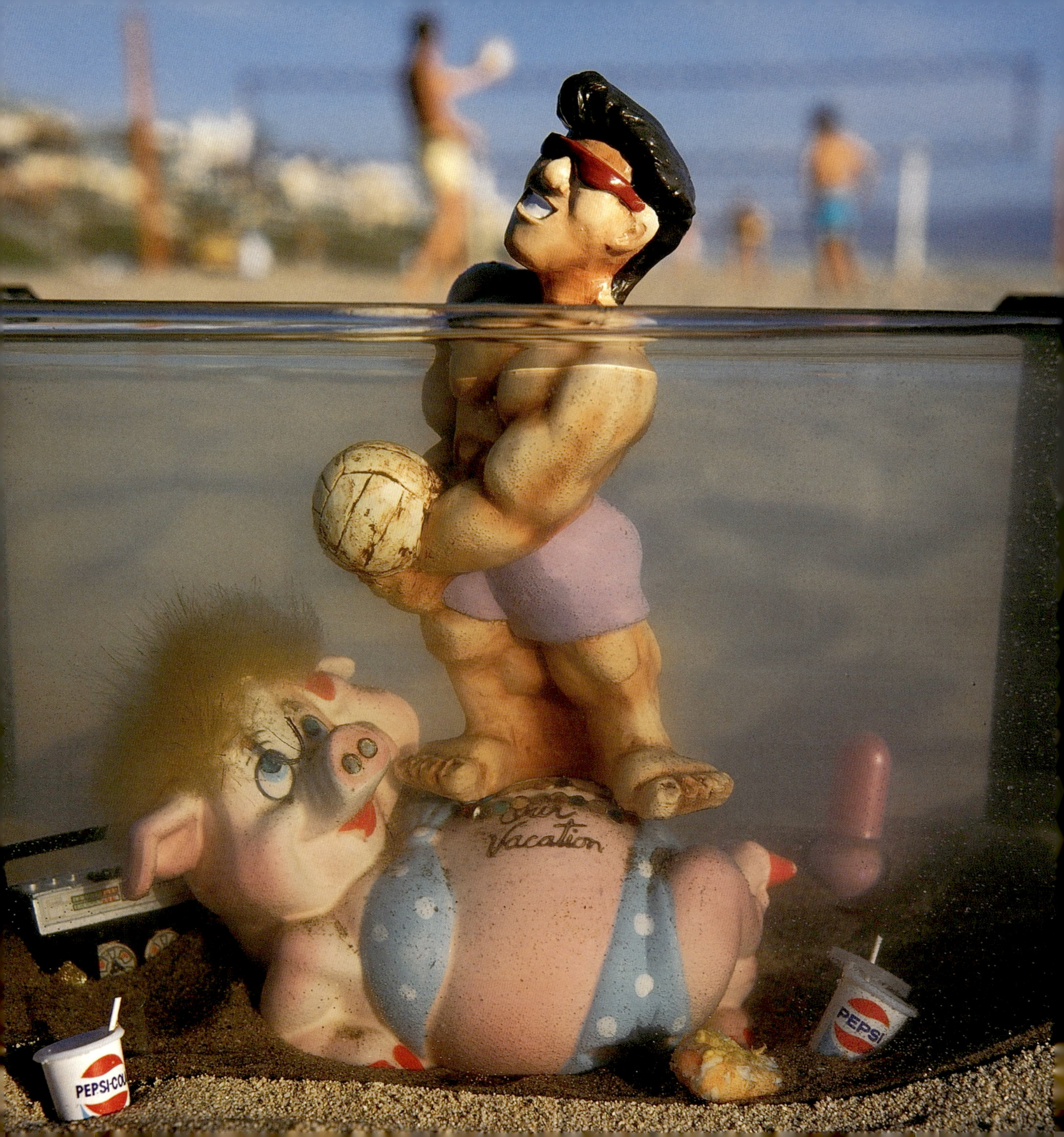
Spring
Vacation
PEPSI-COLA
PEPSI

Be the master of your art—
The greatest can transform
Everyday reality into
Wonders beyond the norm.

30]

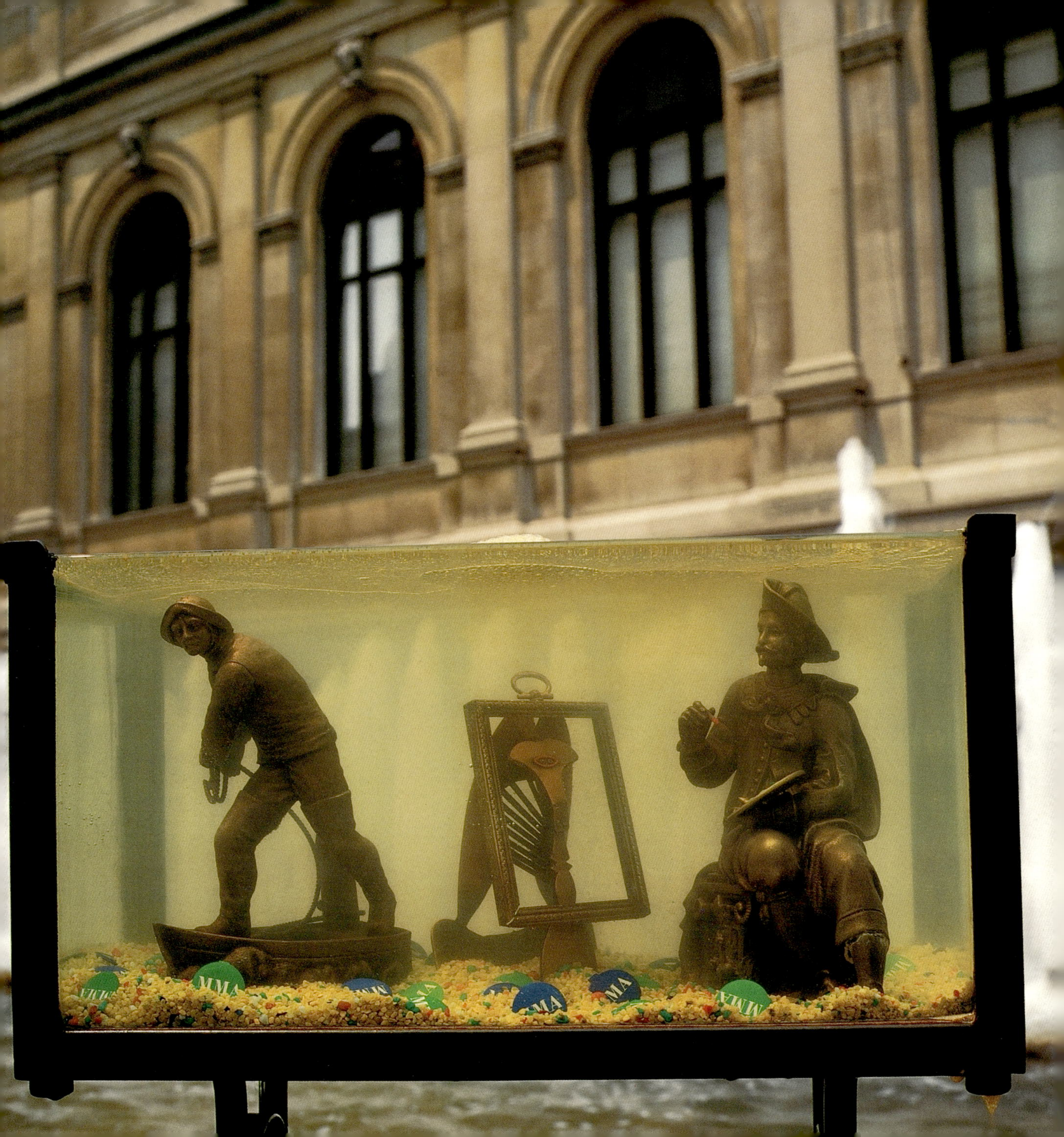

MMA

To make ethereal music,
A teacher can expand a diva's voice
As if her singing breath
Had not a simple choice.

32]

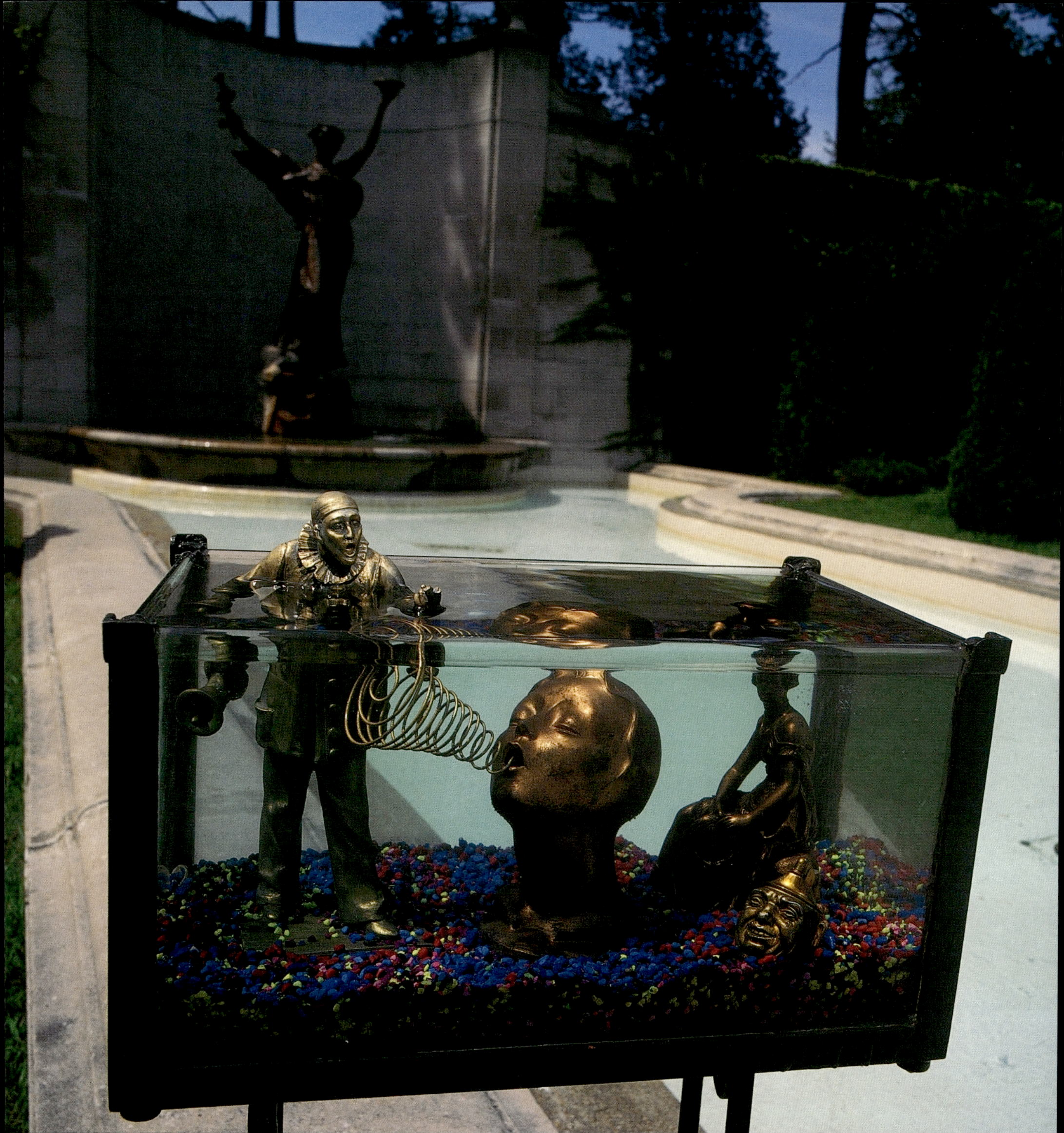

And ultimately you'll be as free
As the newborn babe
Who takes to water instinctively.

34)

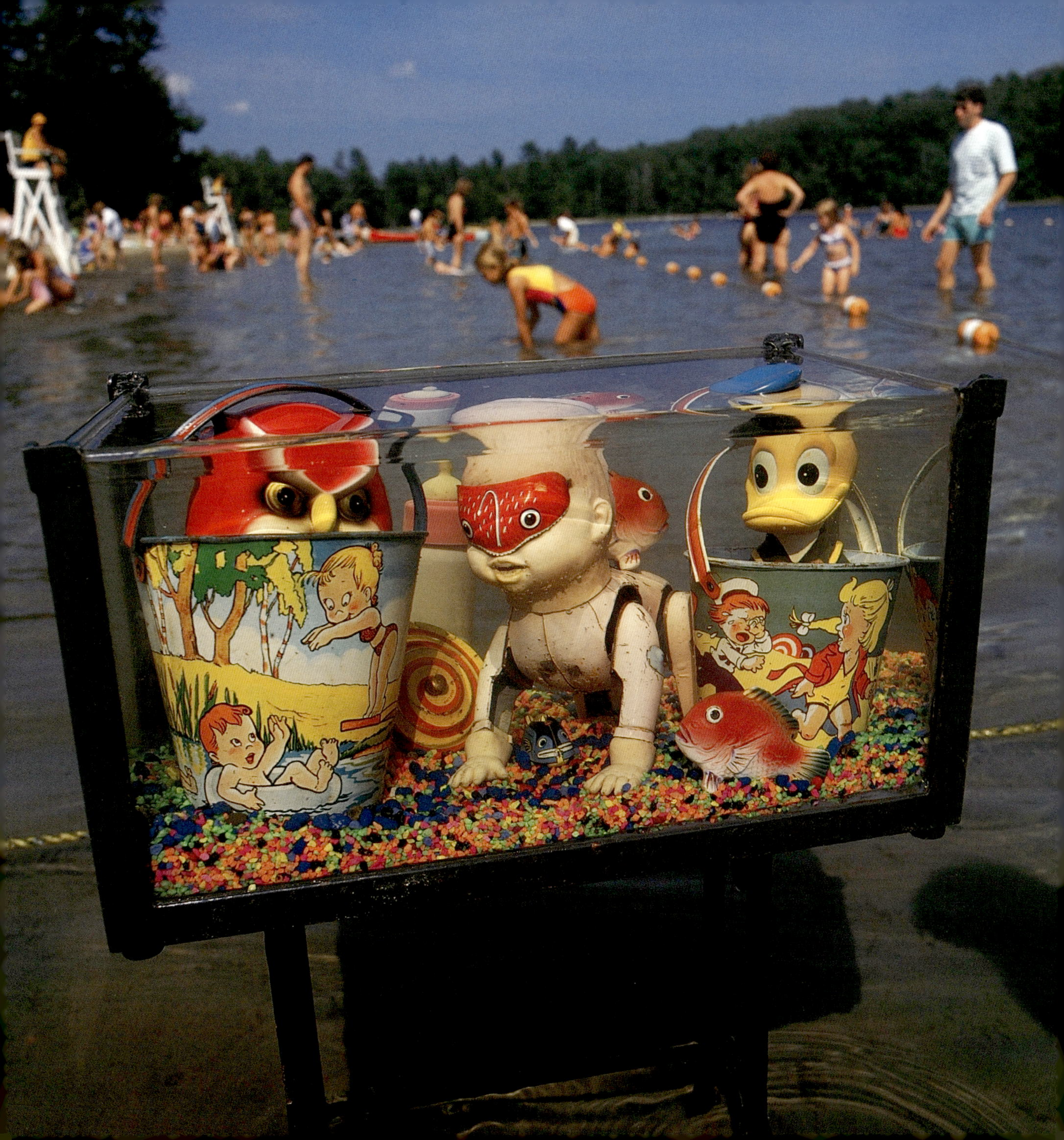

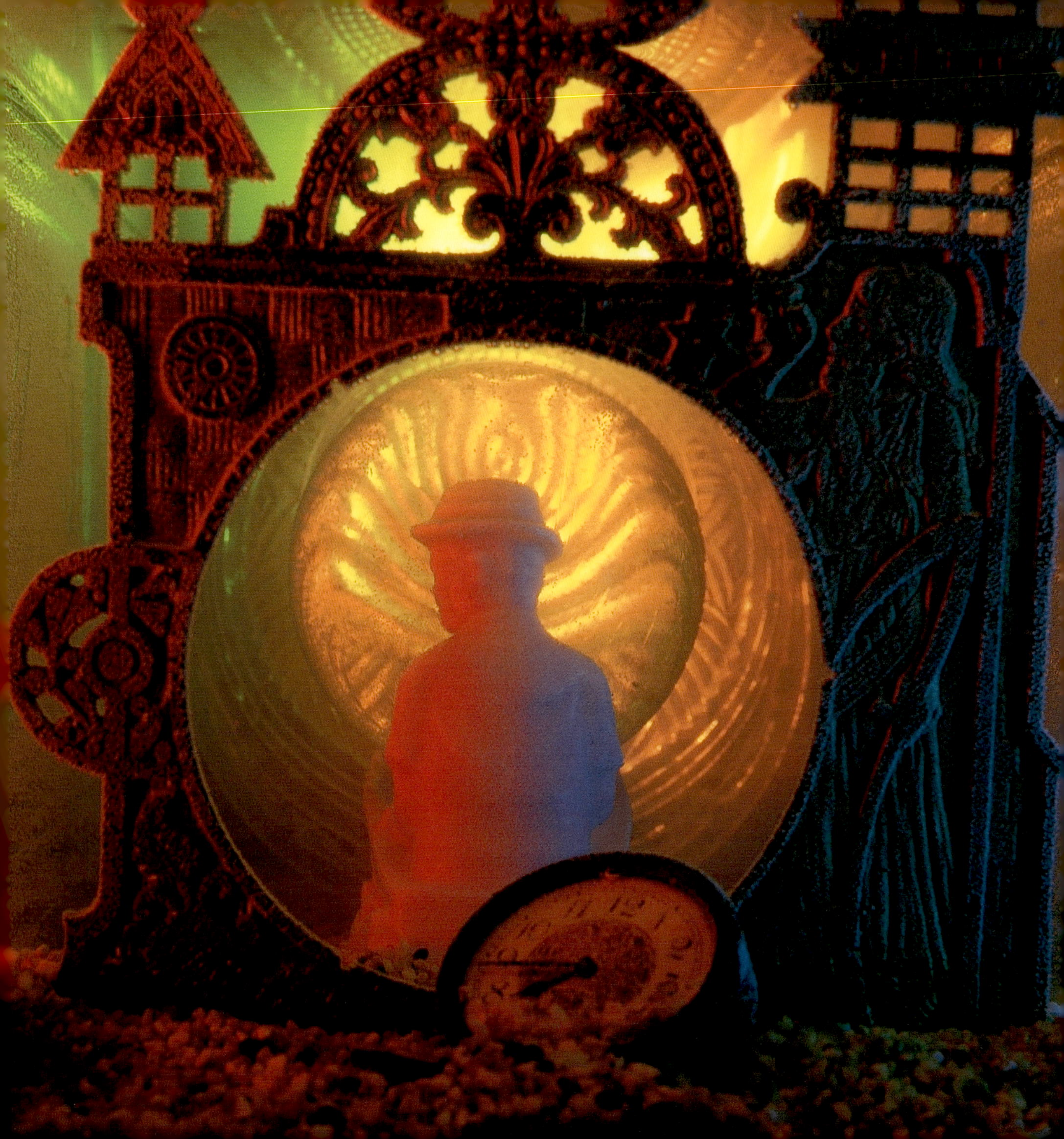

II.
The Depths of Time

Part II, in which the fisherman is taken on a tour of history. He is shown life evolving from the sea, the advent of mankind, and the rise and fall of civilizations. He sees the arrival and departure of political heroes and hears of the untold consequences of corporate optimism and technological progress.

The pages of history
Lend endless instruction
On the rise of all creatures
And their inevitable destruction.

Primordial seas of dazzling variety
Grew thickets of peril
Devoid of false piety.

38]

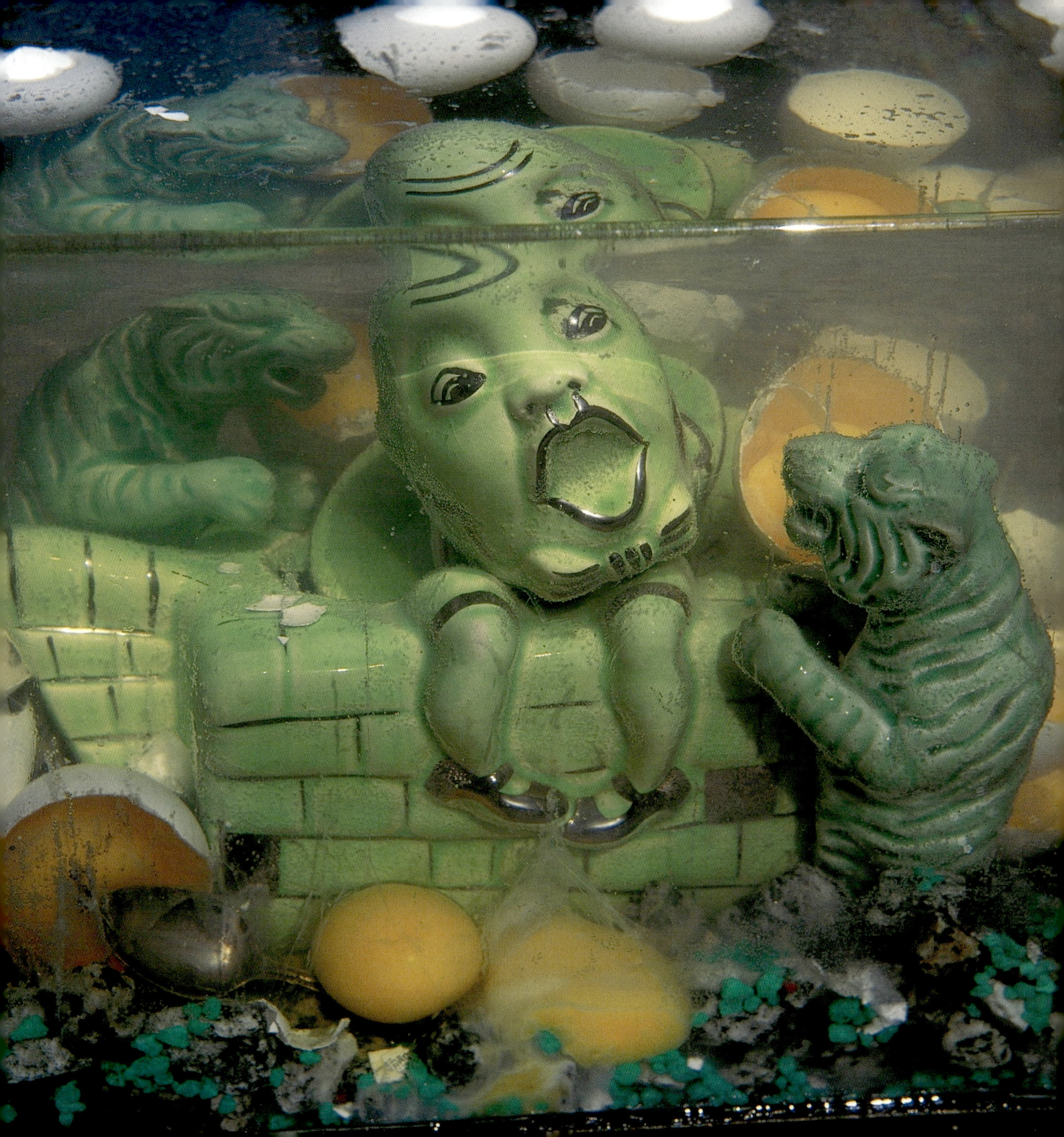

Life bloomed and evolved
With miraculous flair,
Leaving behind ooze
For fresh light and air.

With great effort and luck,
Sea creatures moved onto land
And had a coming-out party
That was ever so grand.

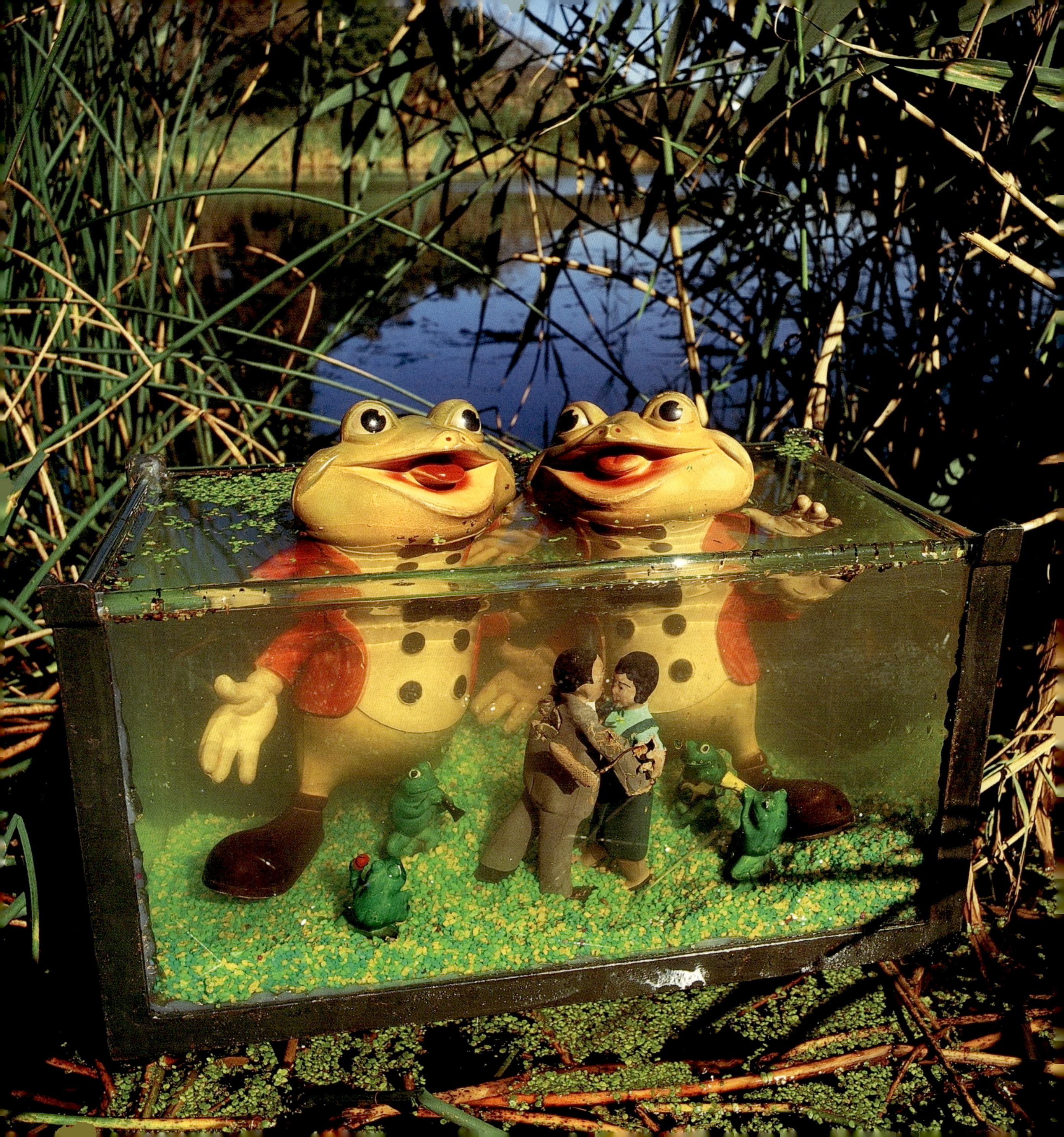

Homo sapiens arrived
To stake out his borders,
Upsetting some established
Natural orders.

Like his animal forebears
But with tools in his hand,
Man built up homes
To cover the land.

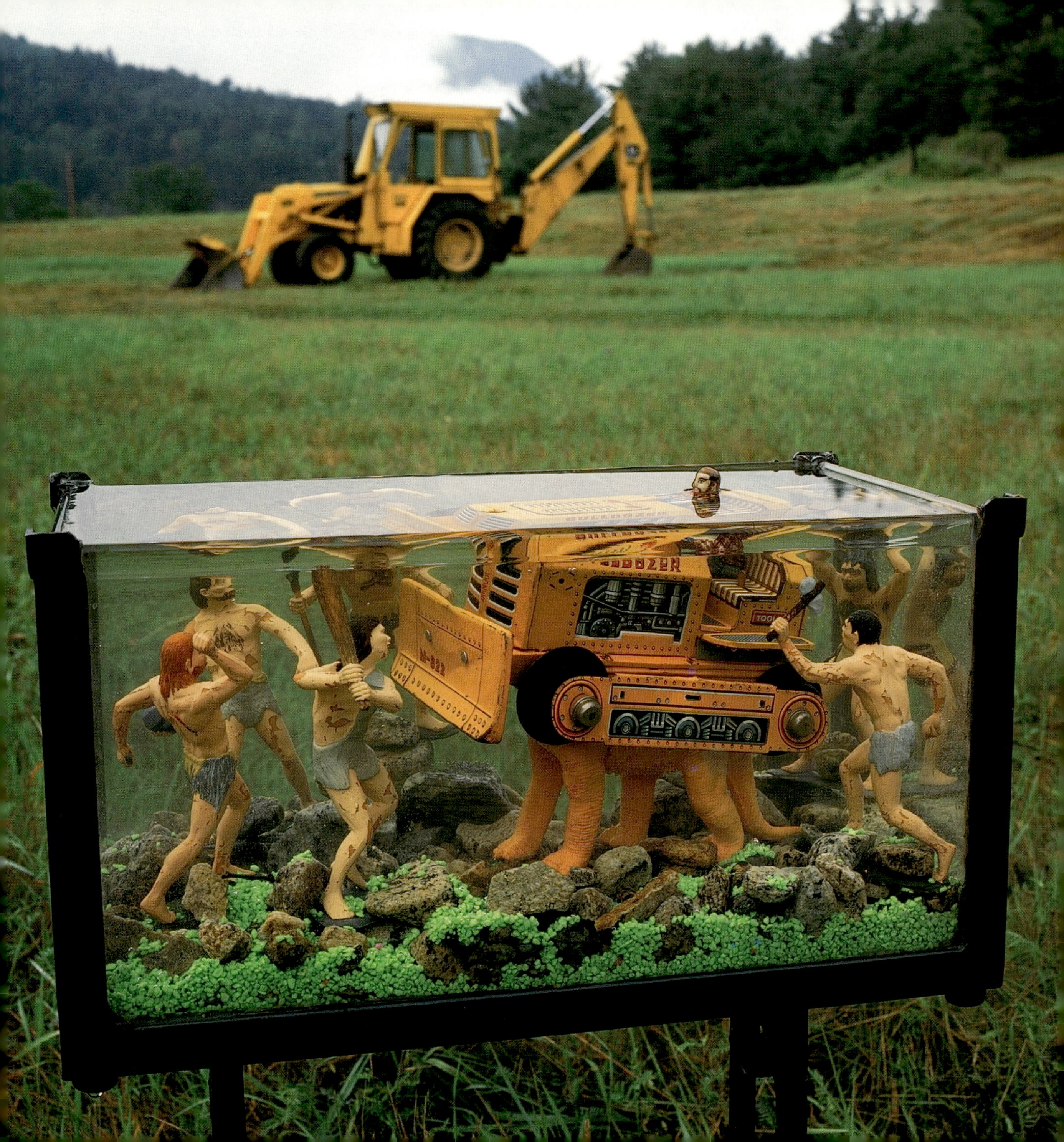
BULLDOZER
M-822
TOOL

Long ago, after combat turned into sport,
The naked wrestlers were givens baths
To soothe those wounds of the civilized sort.

44)

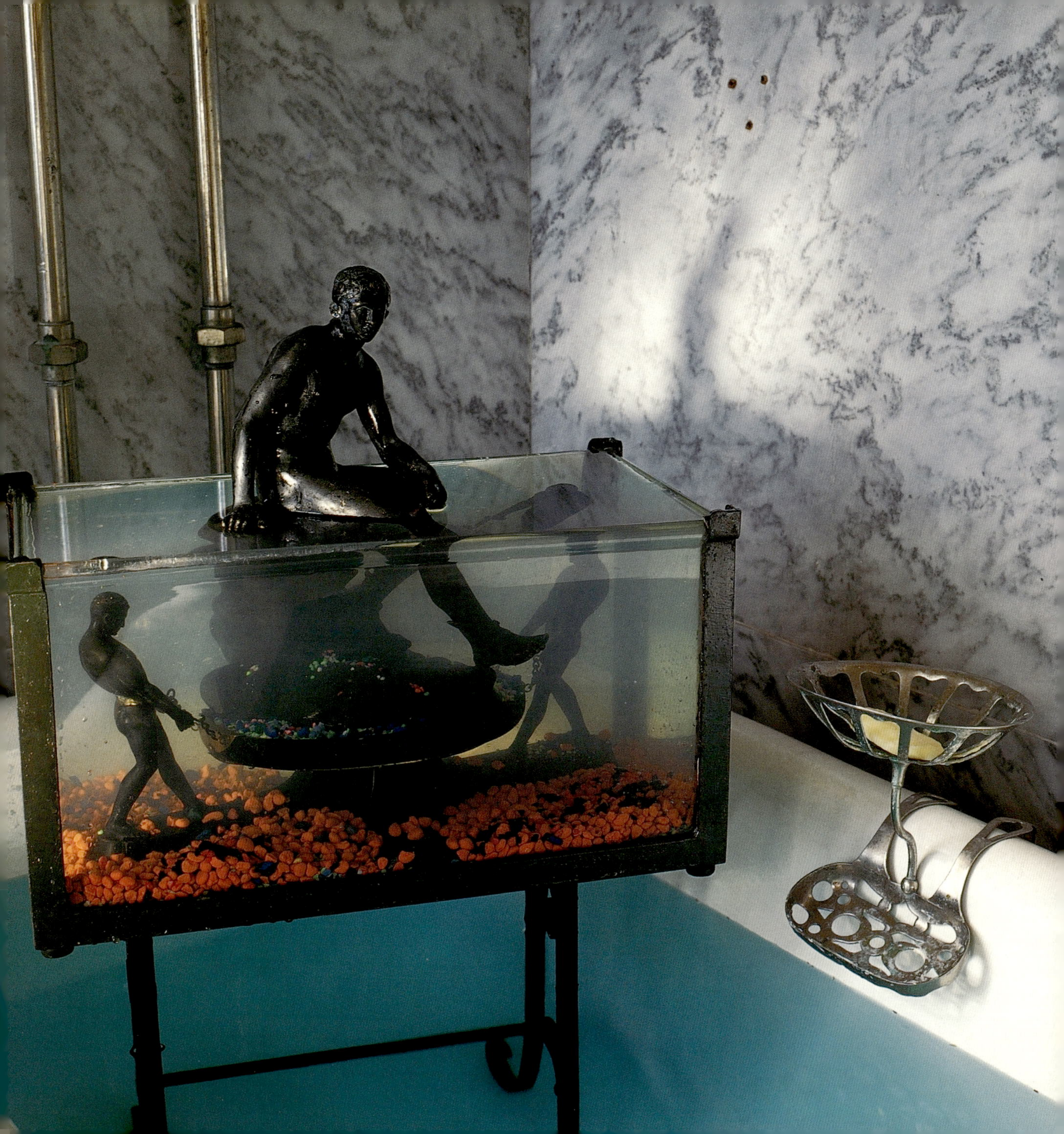

And sport became combat
For the gallant knight
Riding in conquest
And enjoying the fight.

46)

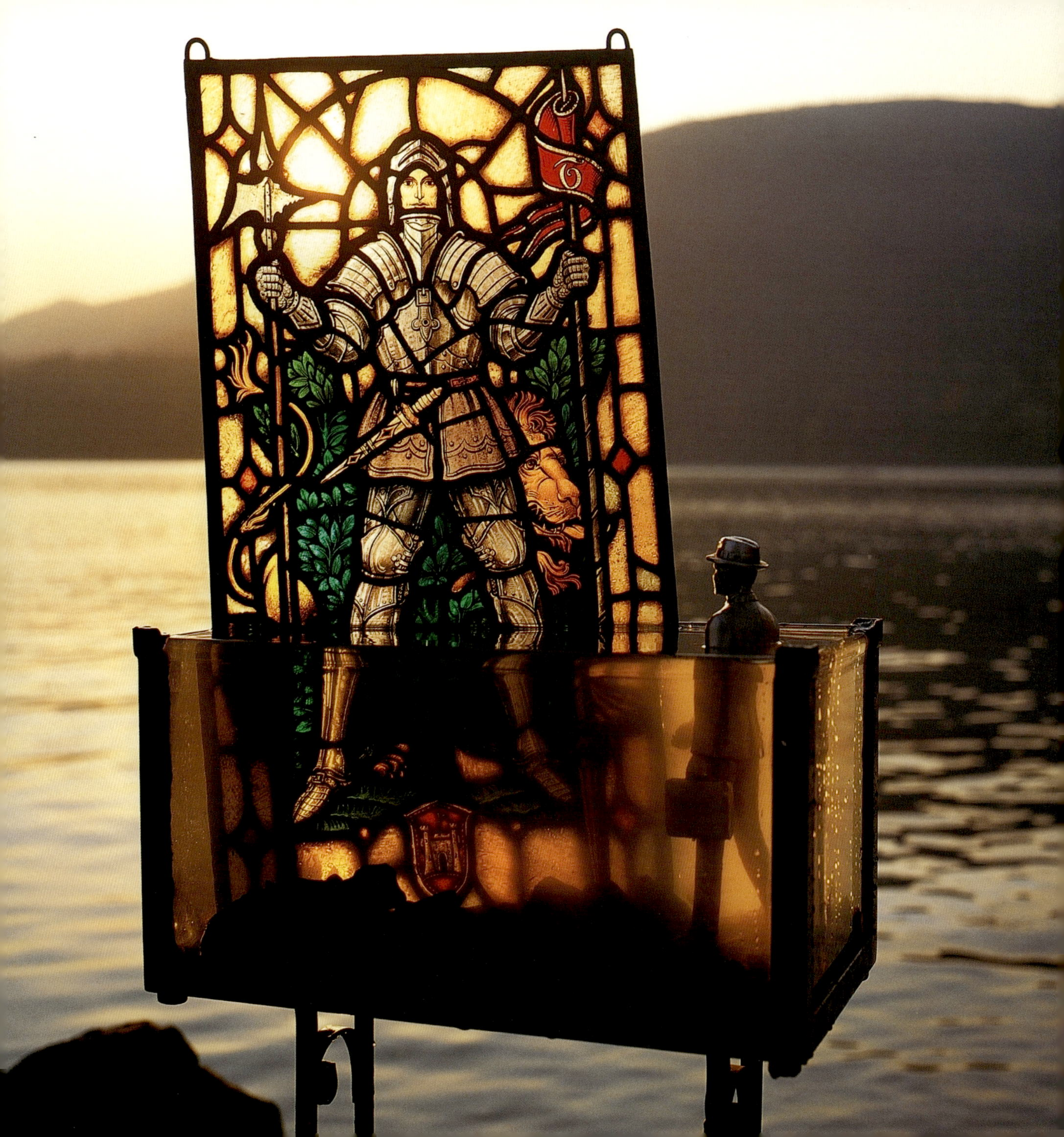

Wise men subjected
The land and the sea
To scientific research's
Brutal scrutiny.

48)

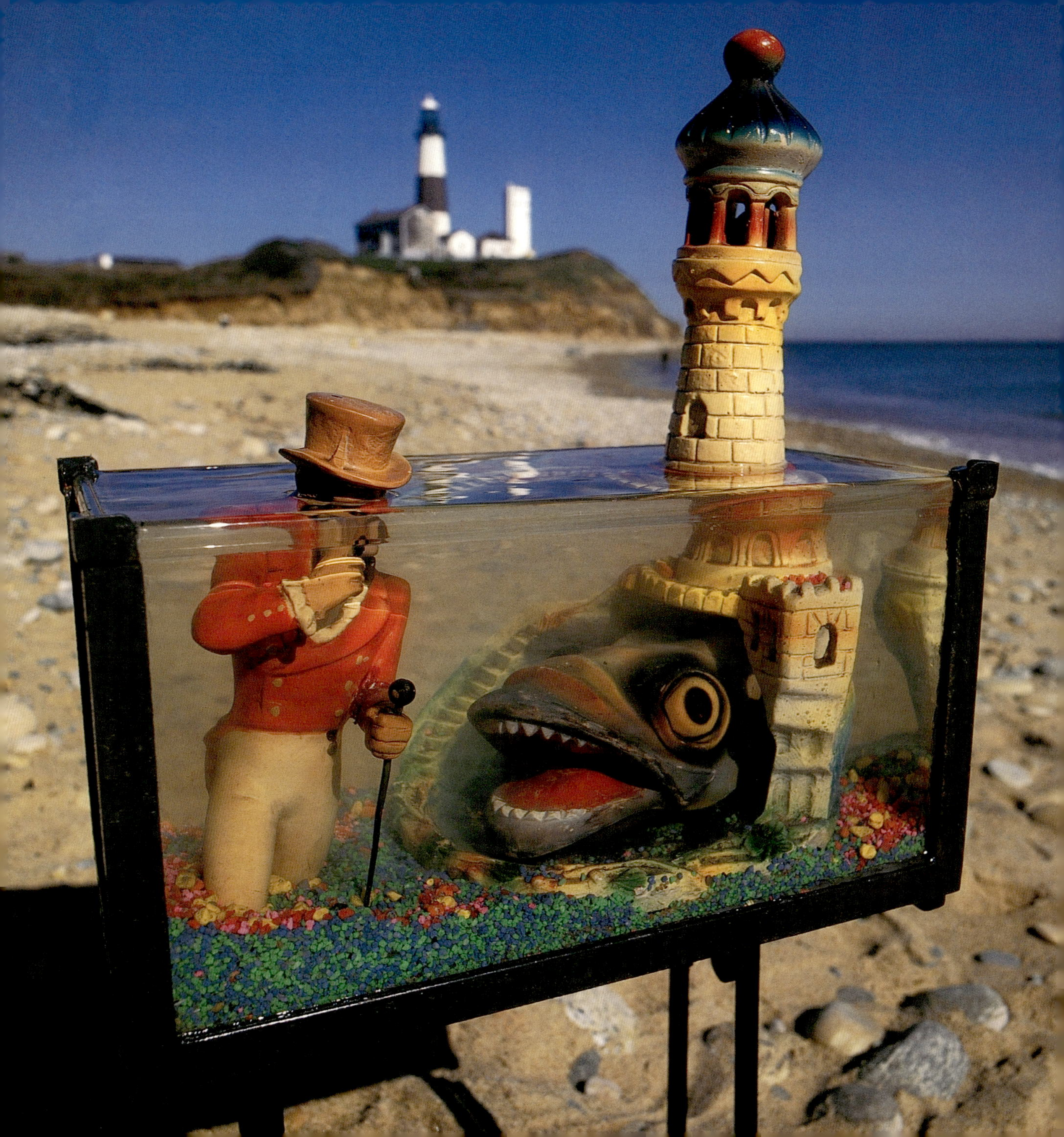

Yet control of the world eluded them all;
They ended up lonely and gray,
Remembering what love they still could recall,
Trying to remember the words they'd wanted to say.

50)

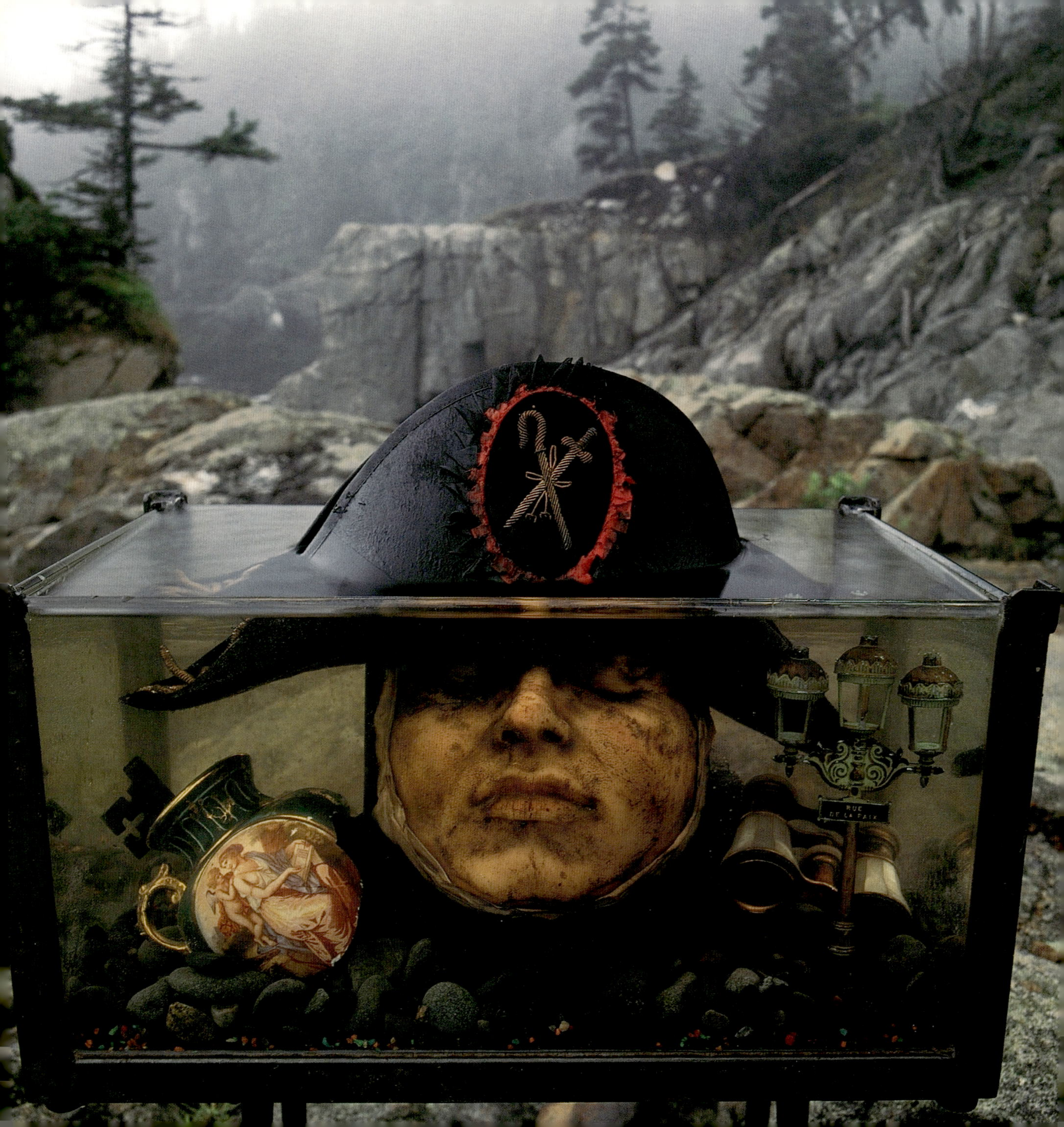
RUE
DE LA PAIX

Generals rallied their people to war
And set out to settle old scores,
But the people didn't give a care,
Being bored with the generals' old wars.

52)

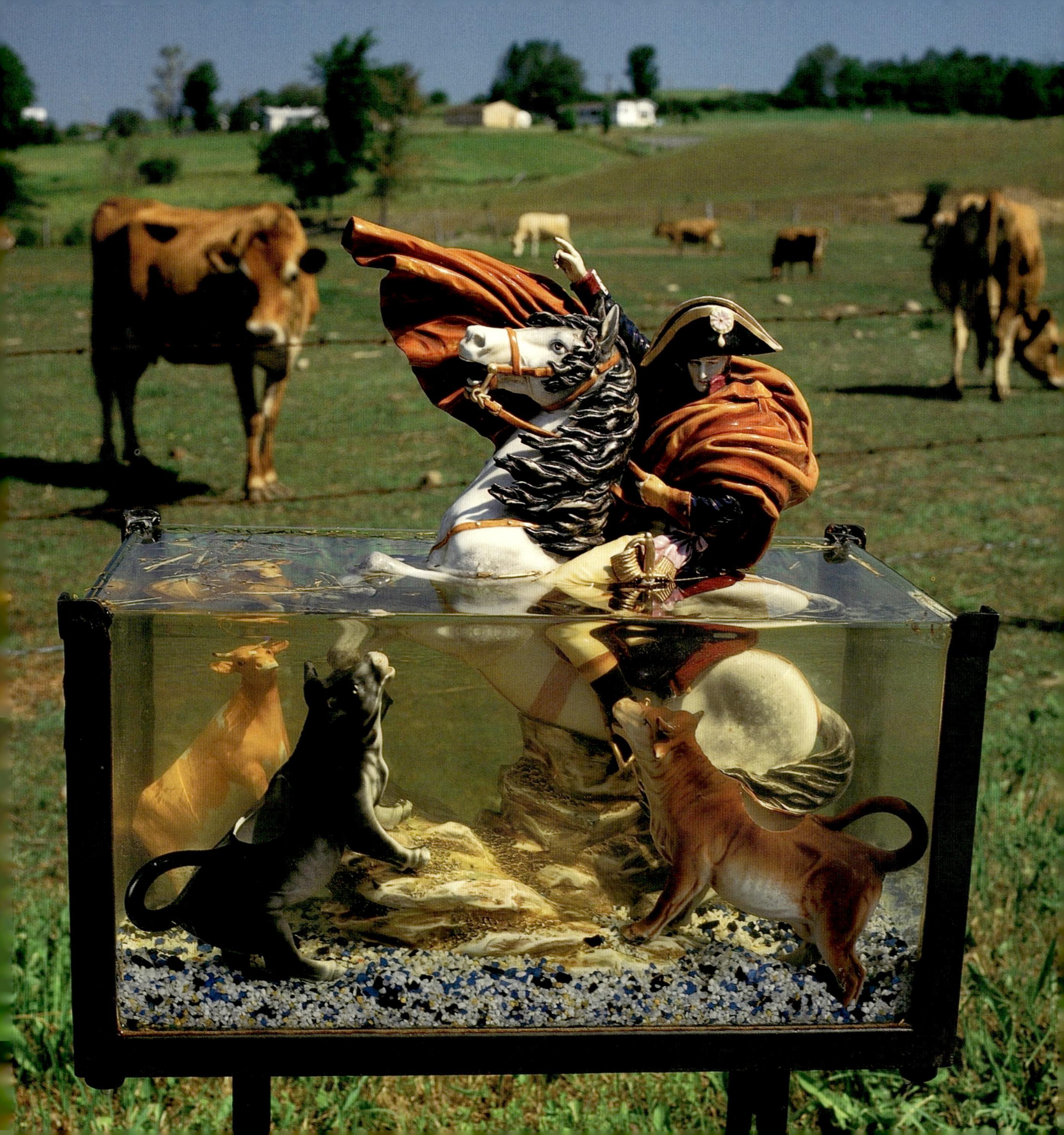

Then governments said, You'll no longer beg;
Our beneficent programs
Will lay golden eggs.

54)

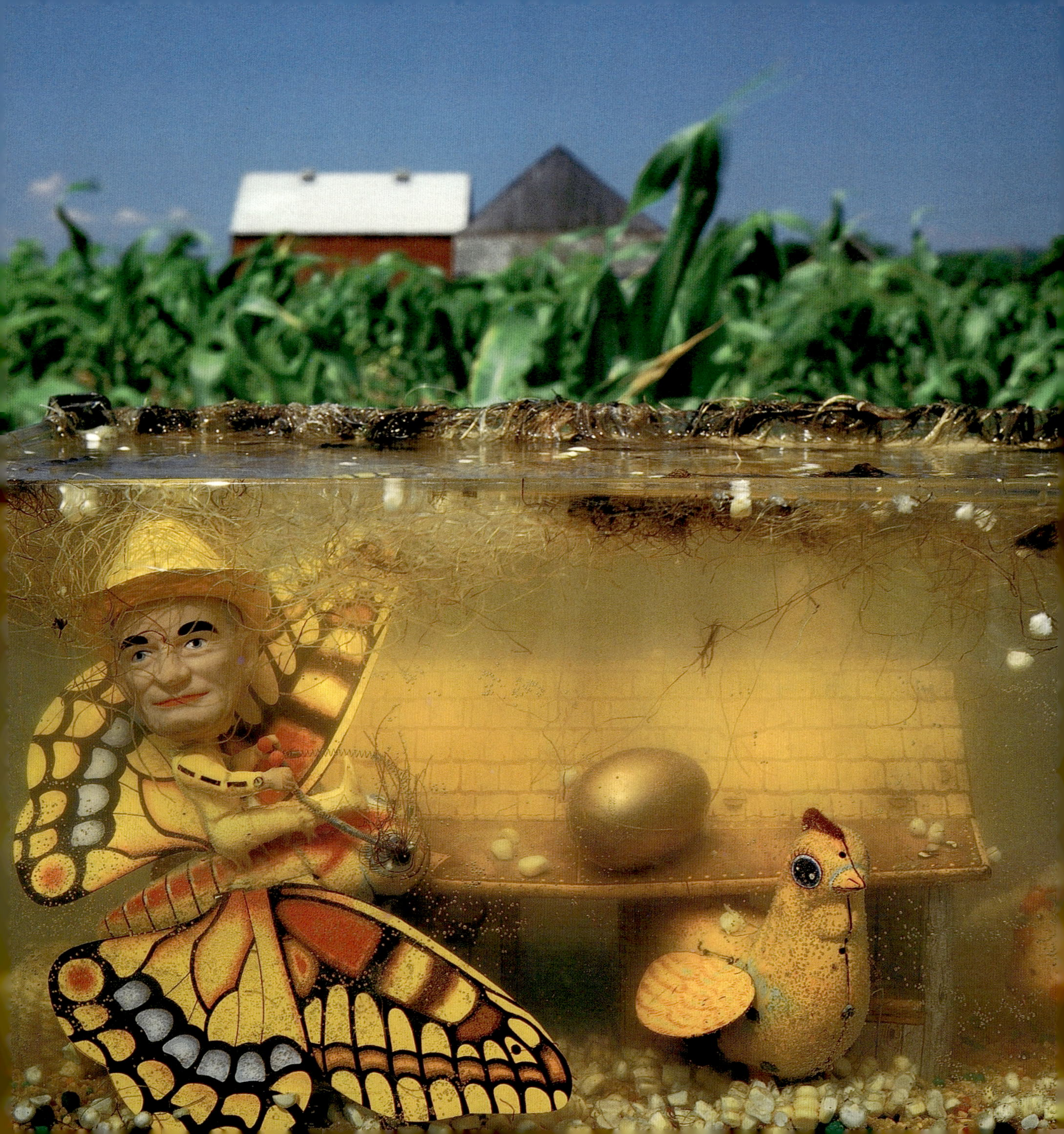

But bureaucrats gained power
And armies flourished
While the rest of the nation
Remained undernourished.

56)

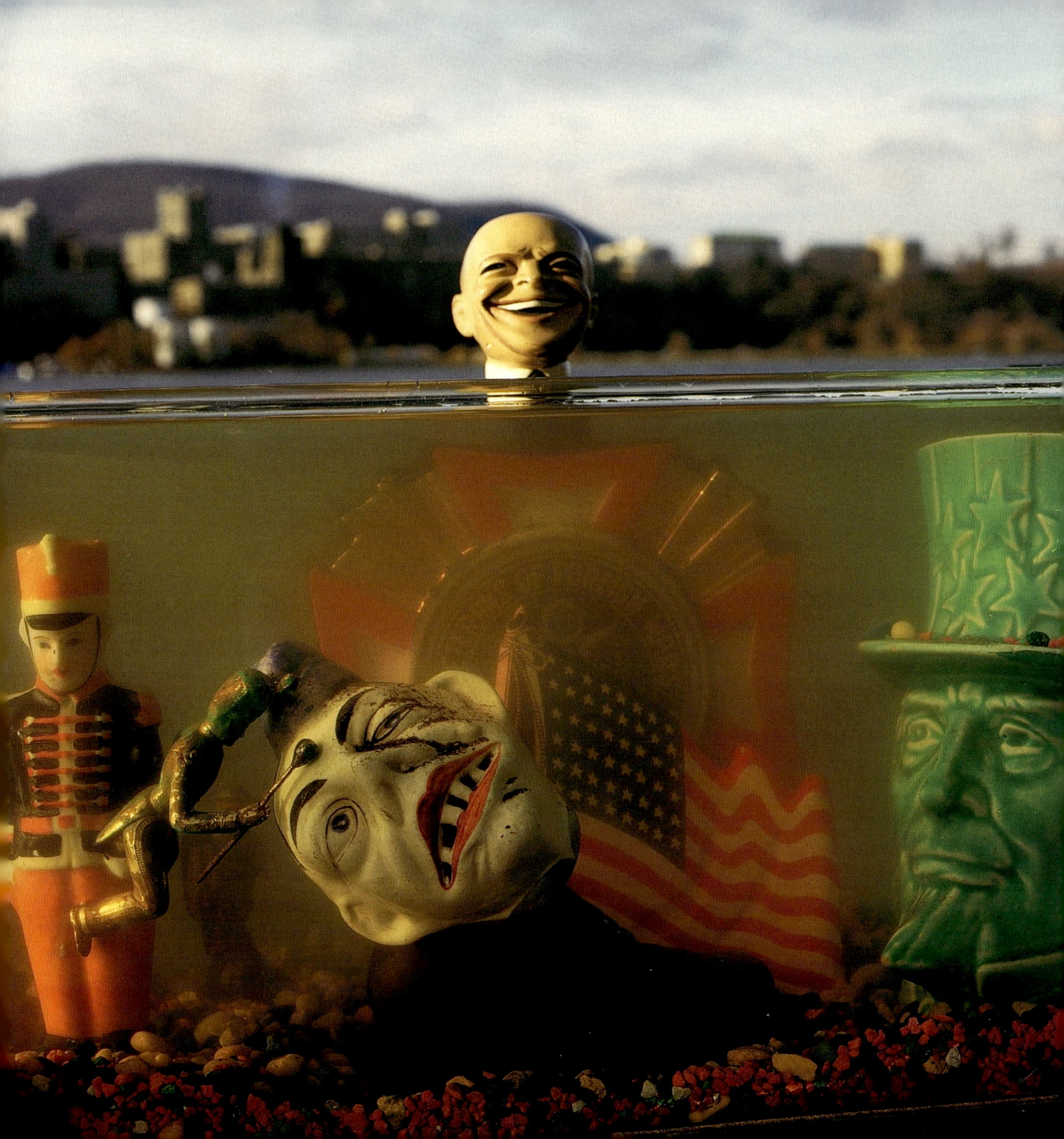

Corporate executives
With fervid inanity
Removed from commerce
All trace of humanity.

58]

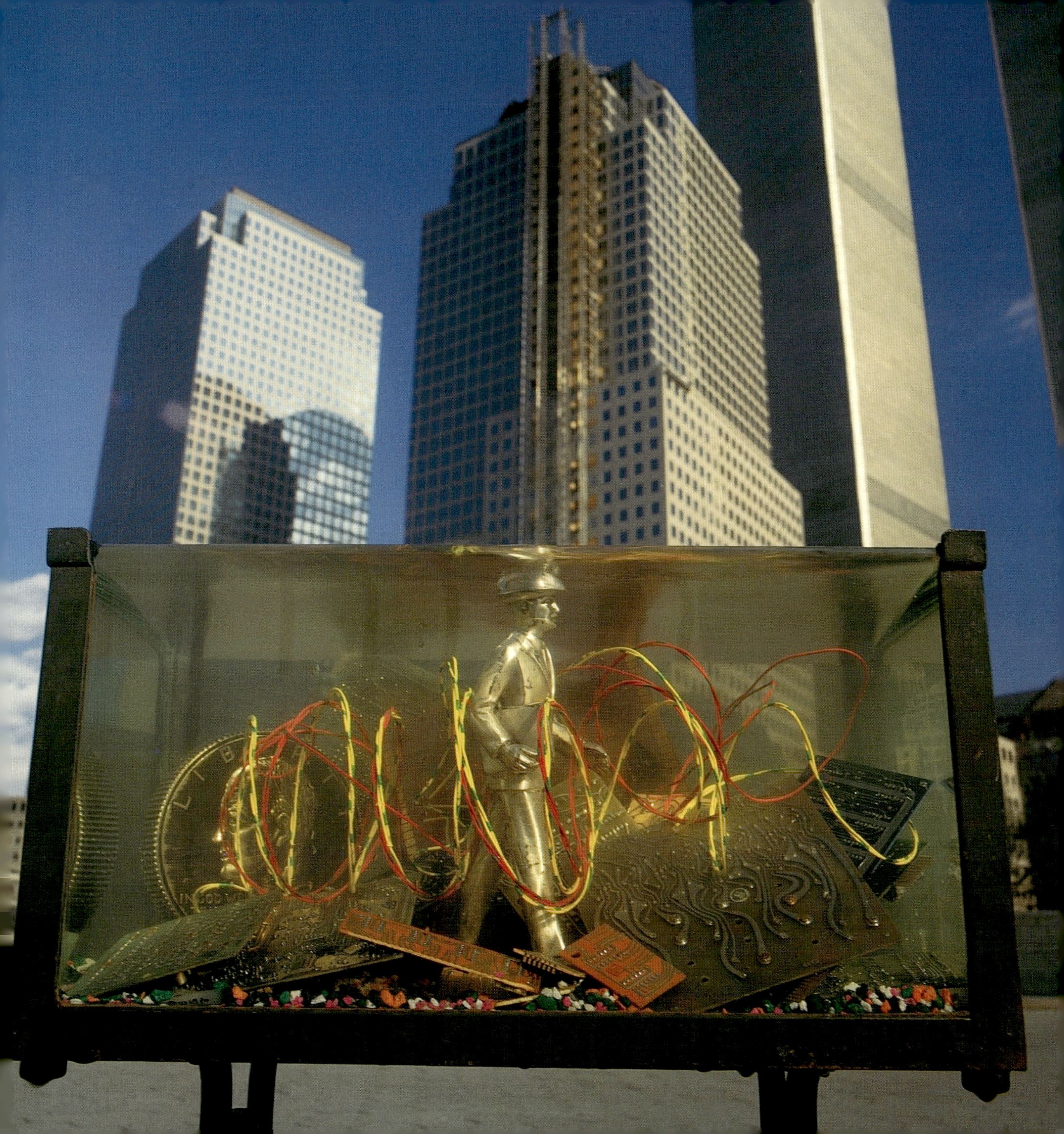

Their cause in its essence—
To promote the efficient—
Brought computers to replace them:
So sadly deficient.

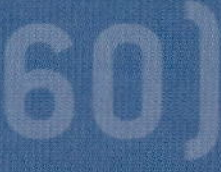

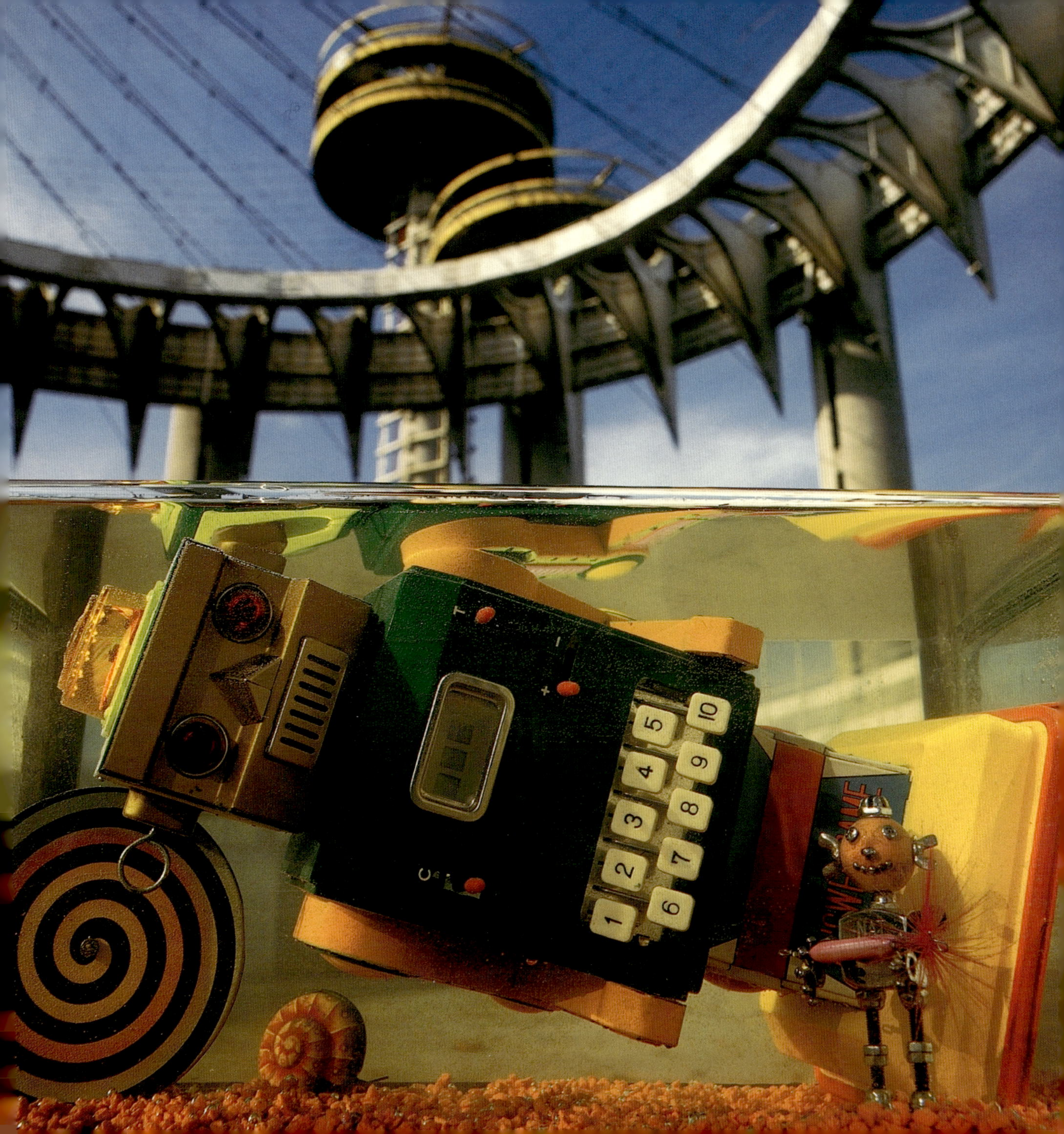

Synthesized food and
Rockets to the moon—
Man's rapid advances
May soon be his ruin.

62]

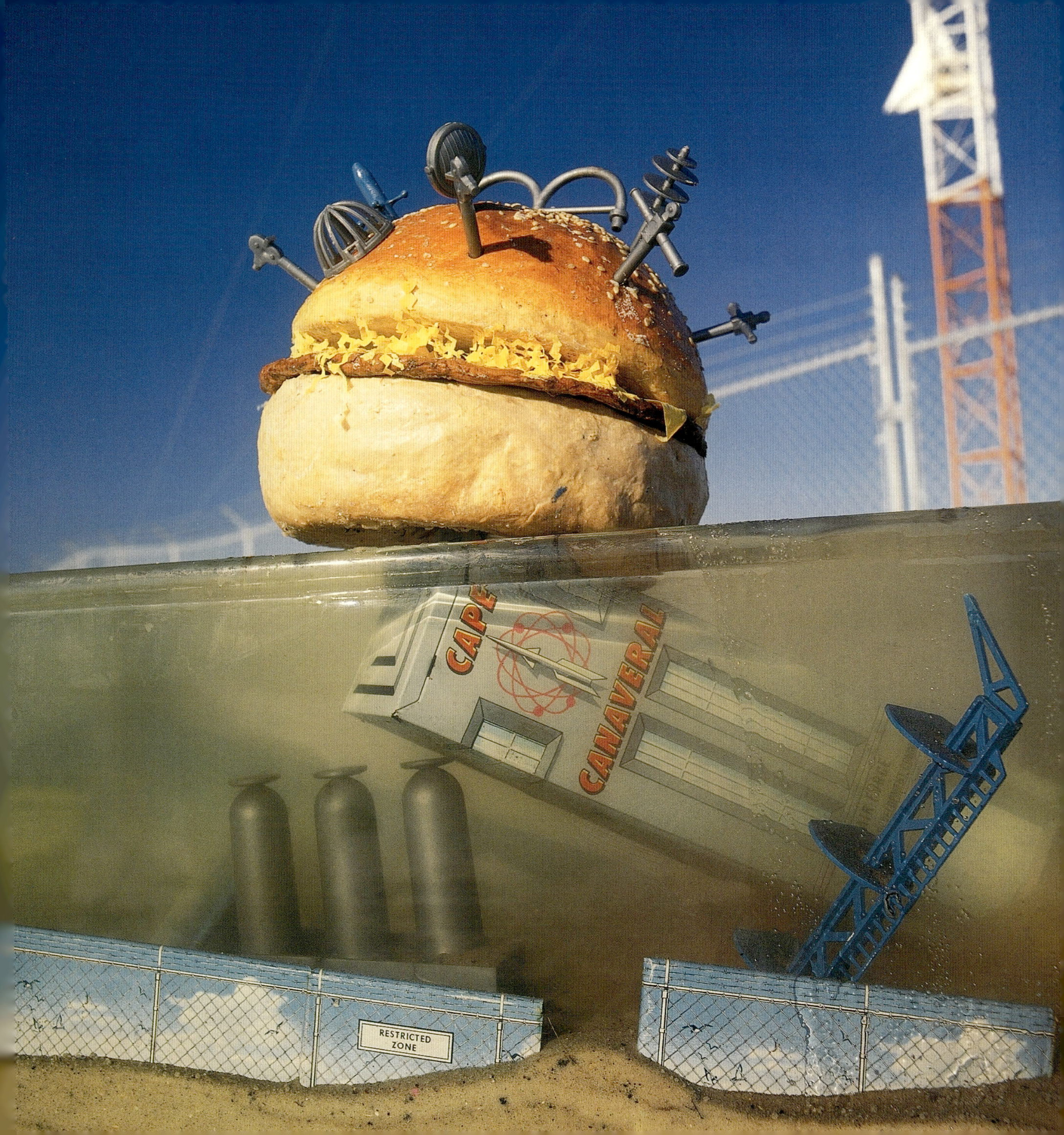

CAPE
CANAVERAL
RESTRICTED ZONE

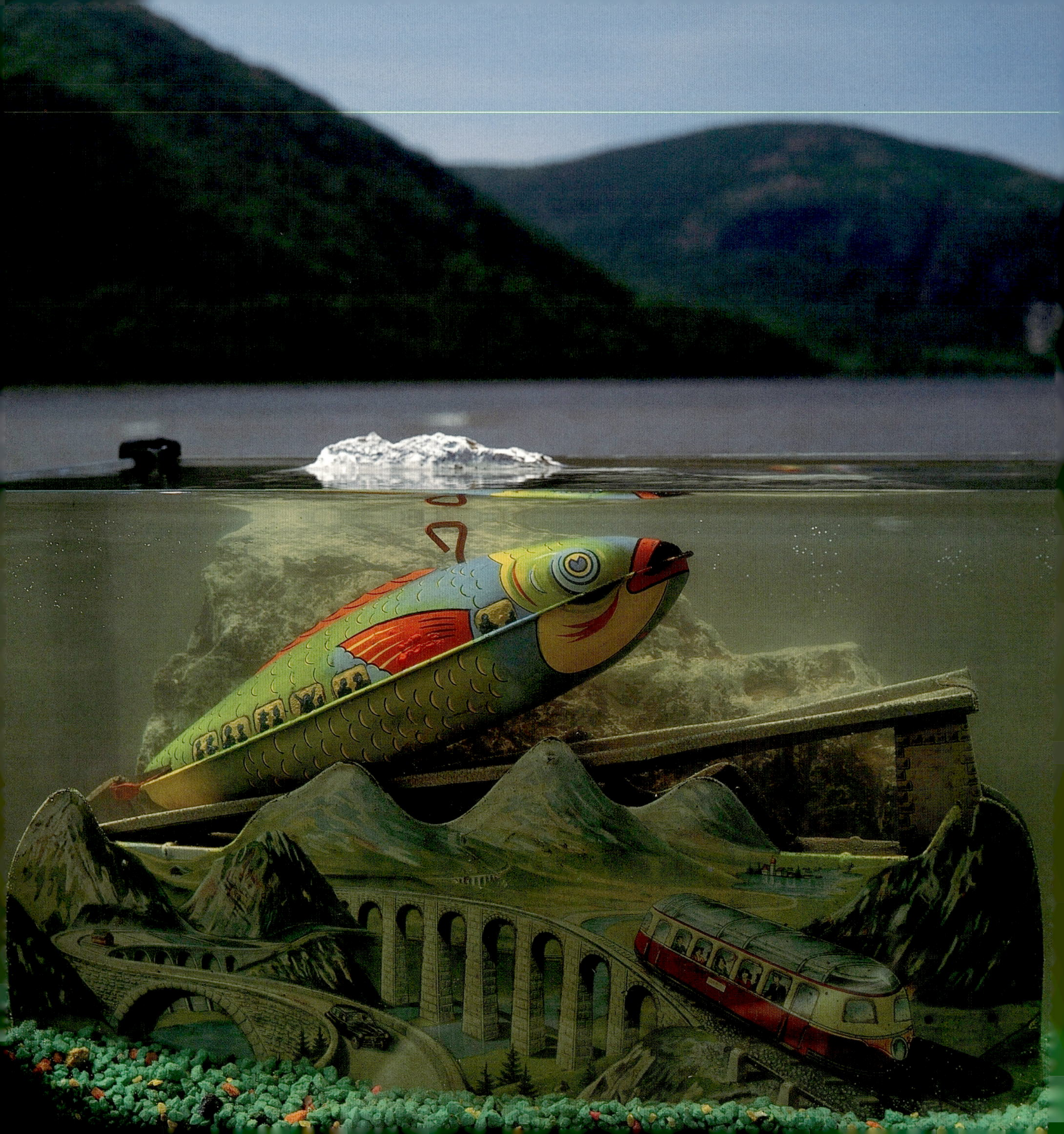

III.
Underworld Underwater

As Part III unfolds, the fisherman is taken on a ride
through the Underworld, where he is shown what fates
befall those who have gone against the natural order.
He experiences the terror of the sportsman's nightmare
when prey becomes hunter, and hunter prey. And he soon
learns that to redress the balance, he must not exceed
his fair share.

Like a weary commuter
Exhausted from strife,
You'll descend on a journey
To the dark side of life.

You must pay the ferryman
And he'll take you across
The stygian waters to
The Islands of the Lost.

66)

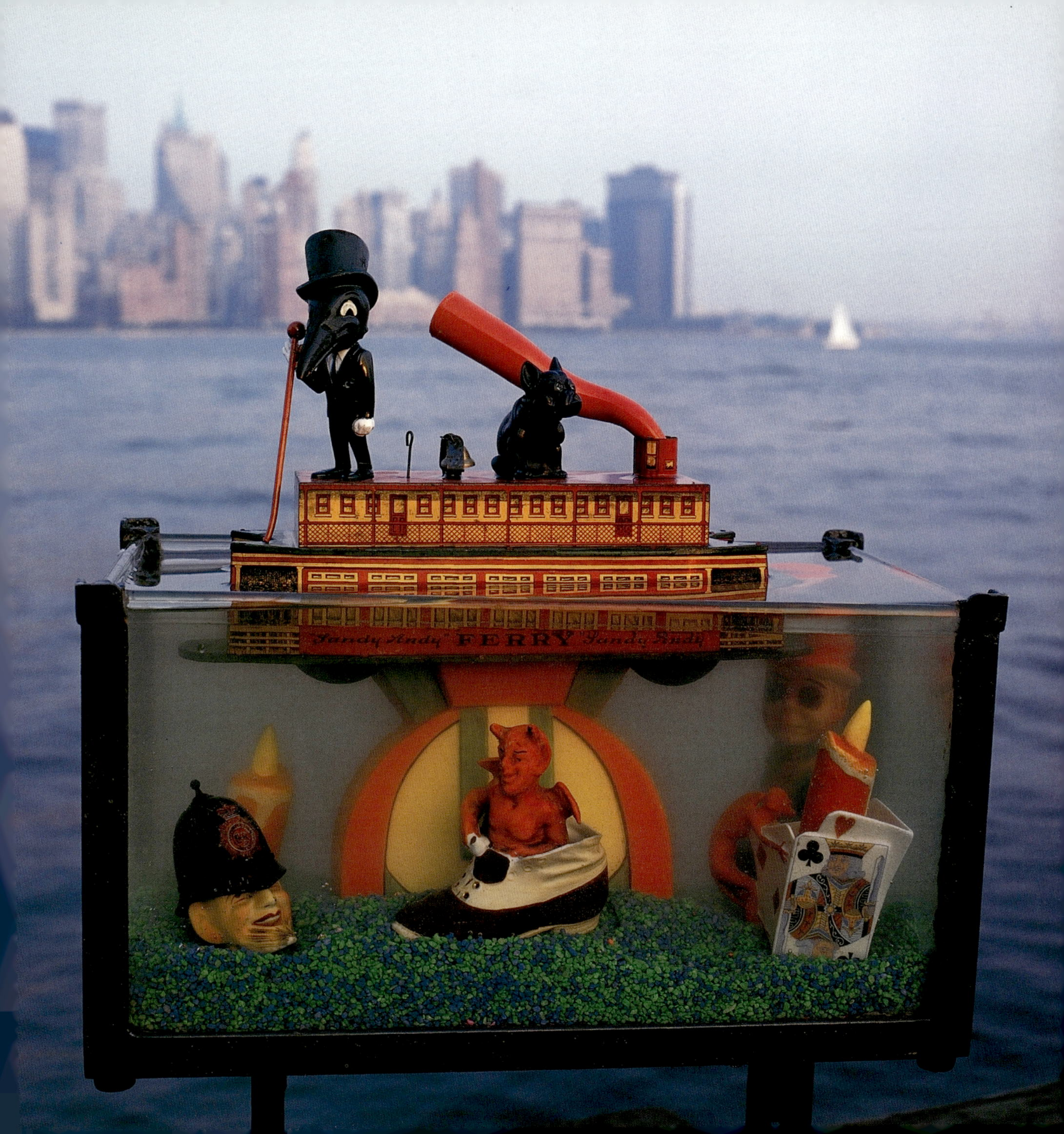

An icy grave, a watery bower
For the titanic liner that scoffed
At the ocean's great power.

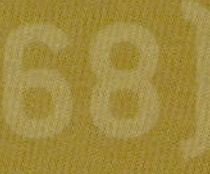

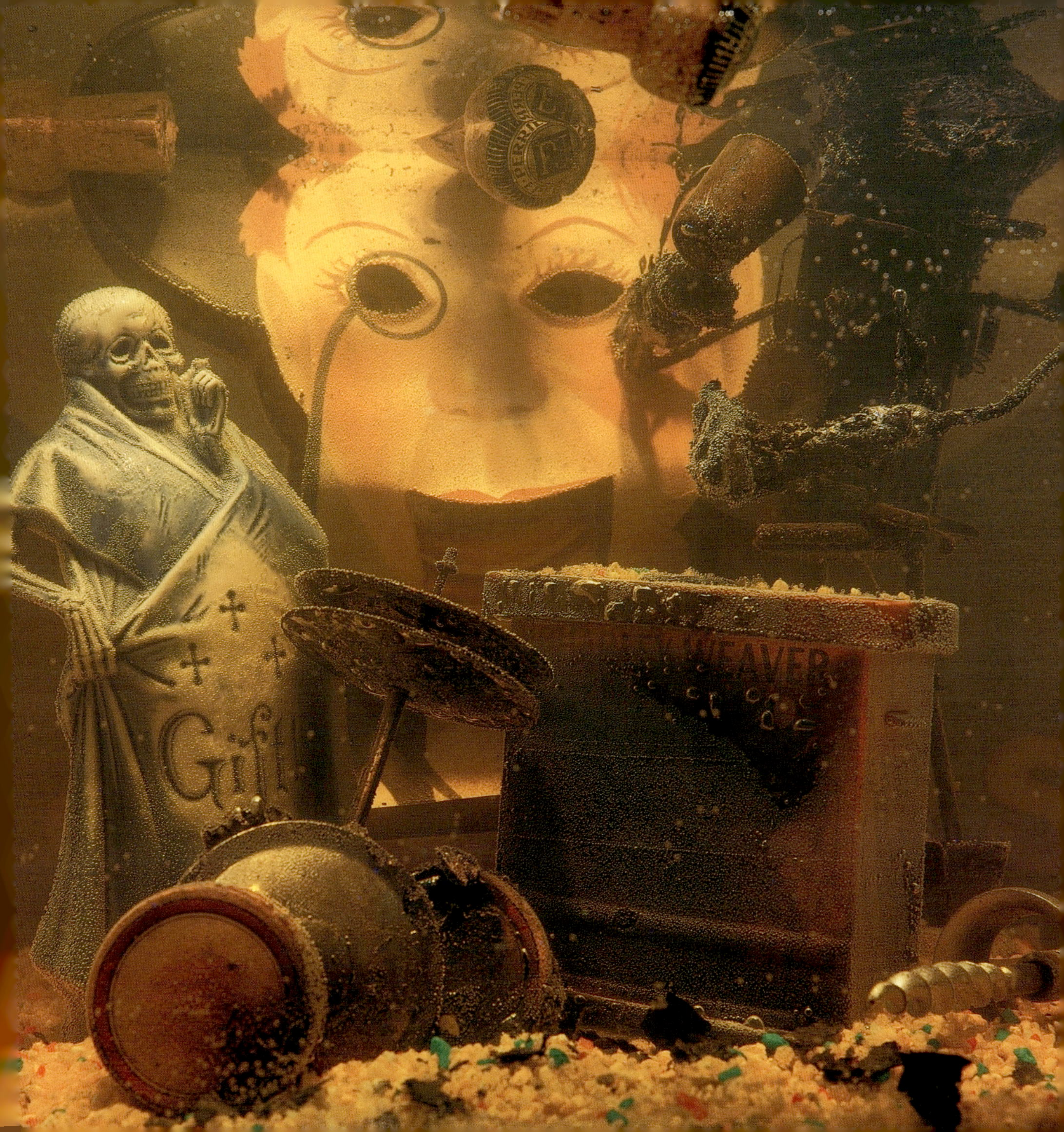
IMPERIAL
Gift
WEAVER

The rich and the cruel
Are immersed, cold and wet,
And kept prisoner here
By their former pets.

70)

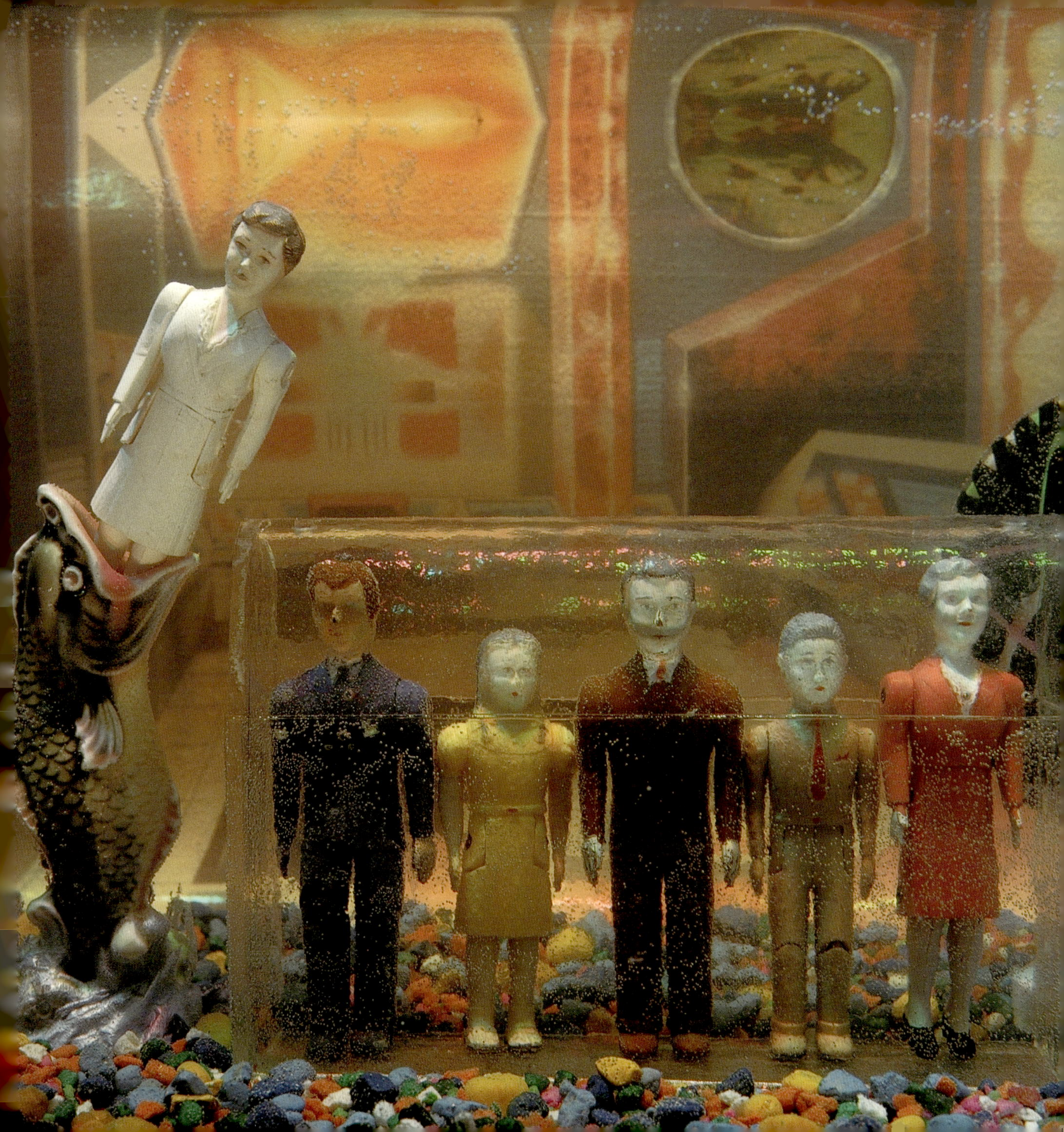

The tank of Stark Insanity
Reserves a special spot
For callous Sunday captains
To race around and rot.

72)

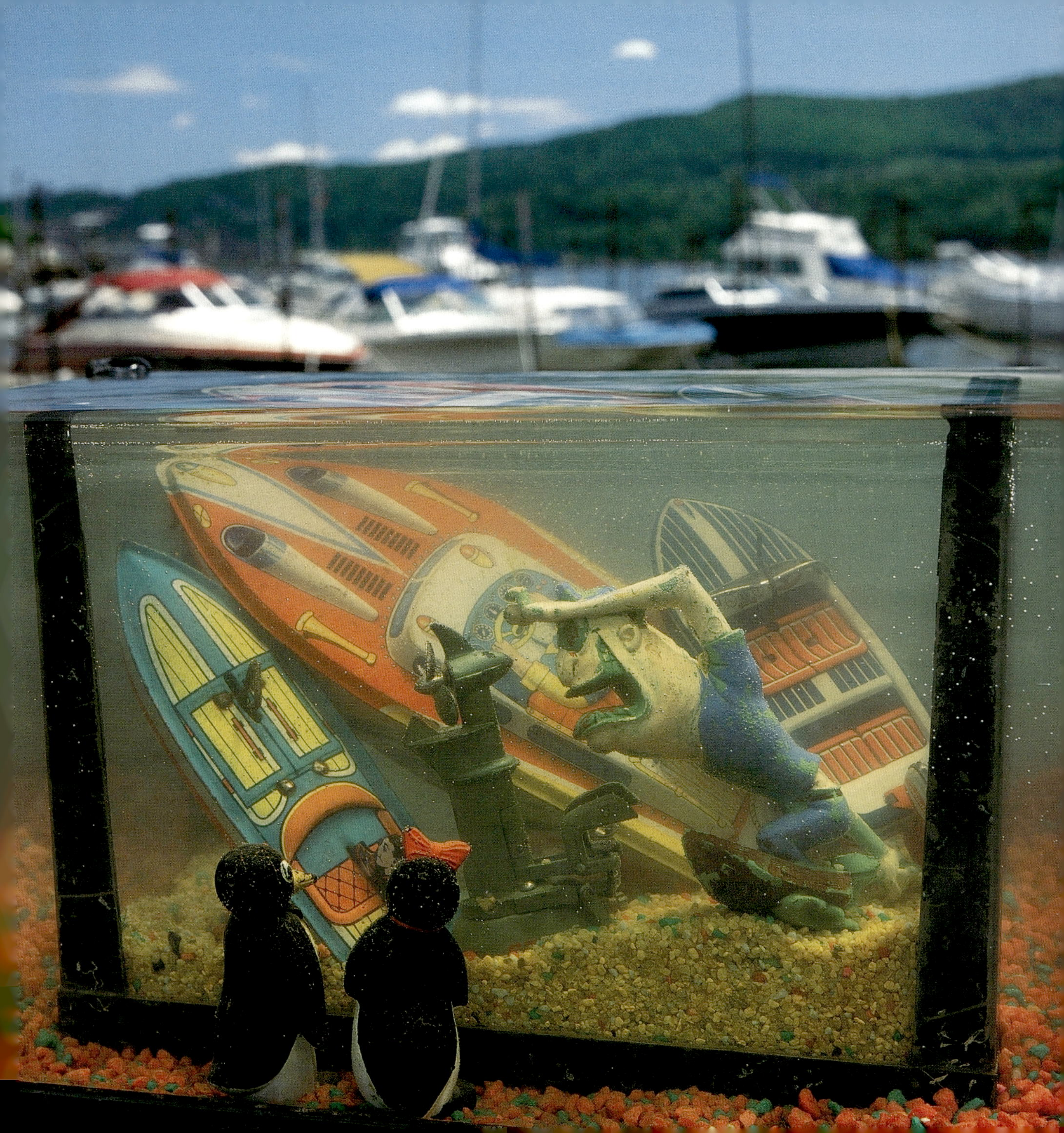

See the cook go down
In the sea of Boiling Stew,
Writhing in the agony
All his lobsters knew.

74)

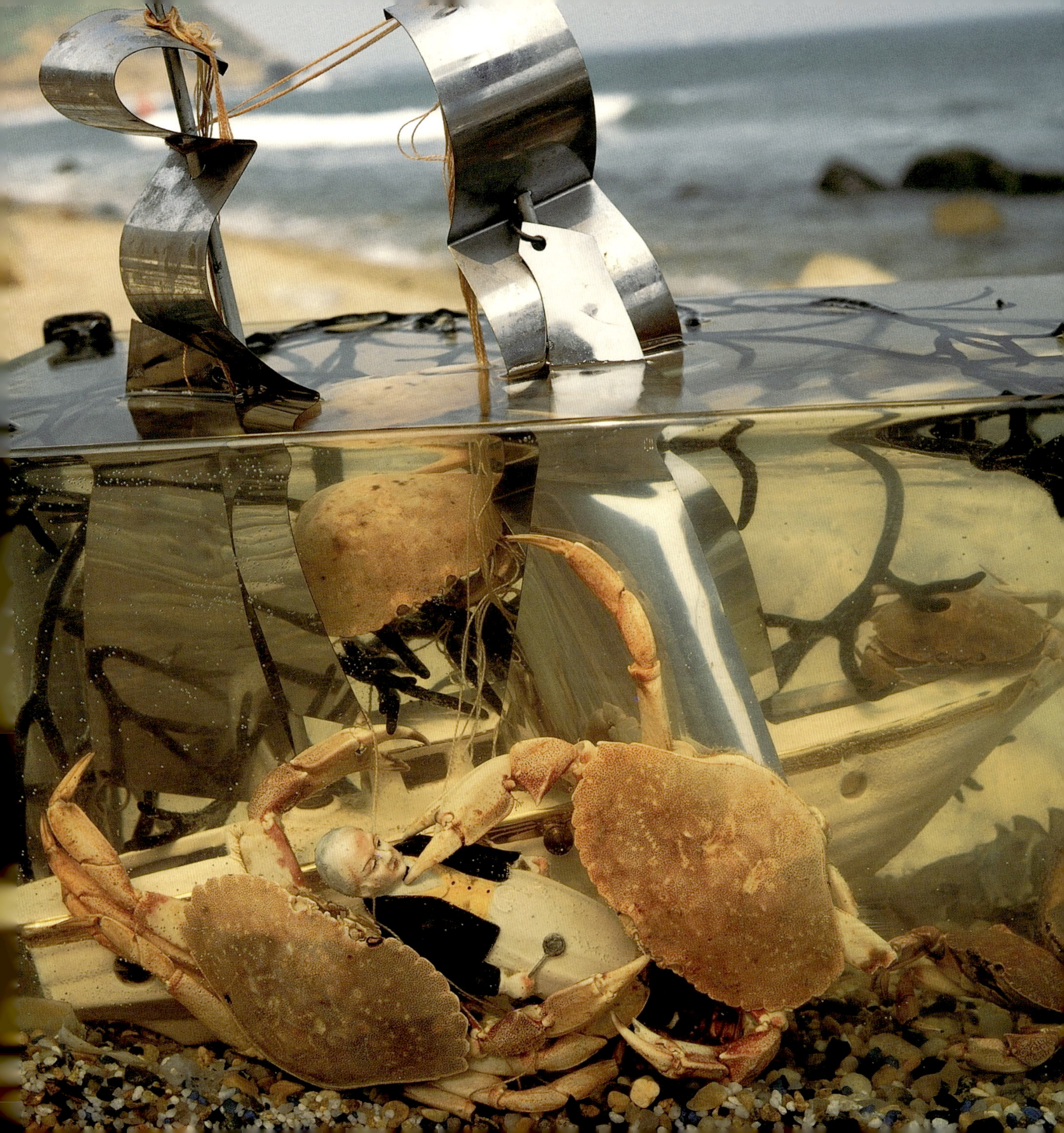

The Lake of Enforcement
Provides a unique solution,
Where unlicensed anglers
Will meet retribution.

76]

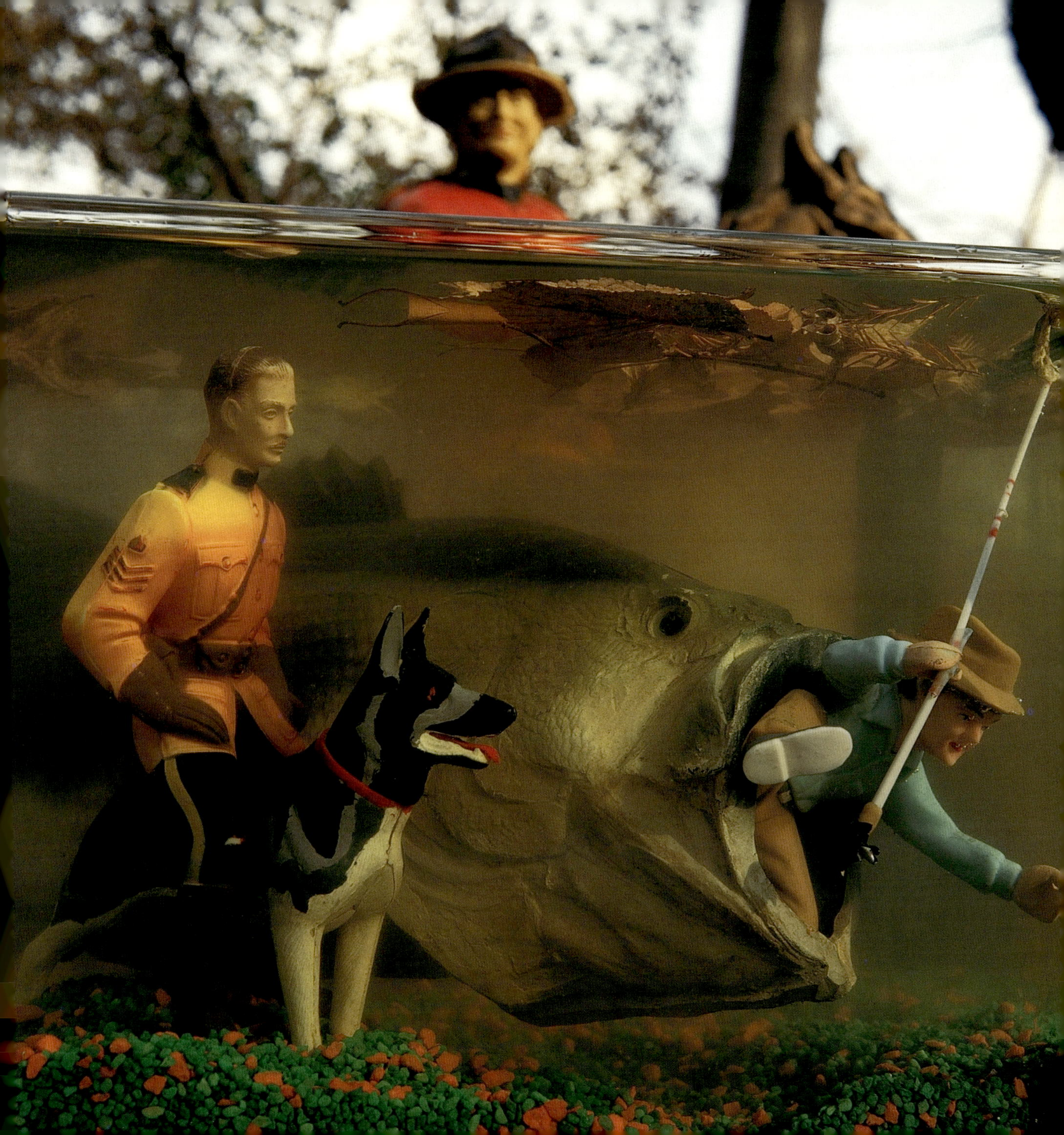

And pity the pusillanimous poodles
In the Pond of Dank Despair;
They once were greedy fishermen
Who exceeded their fair share.

78]

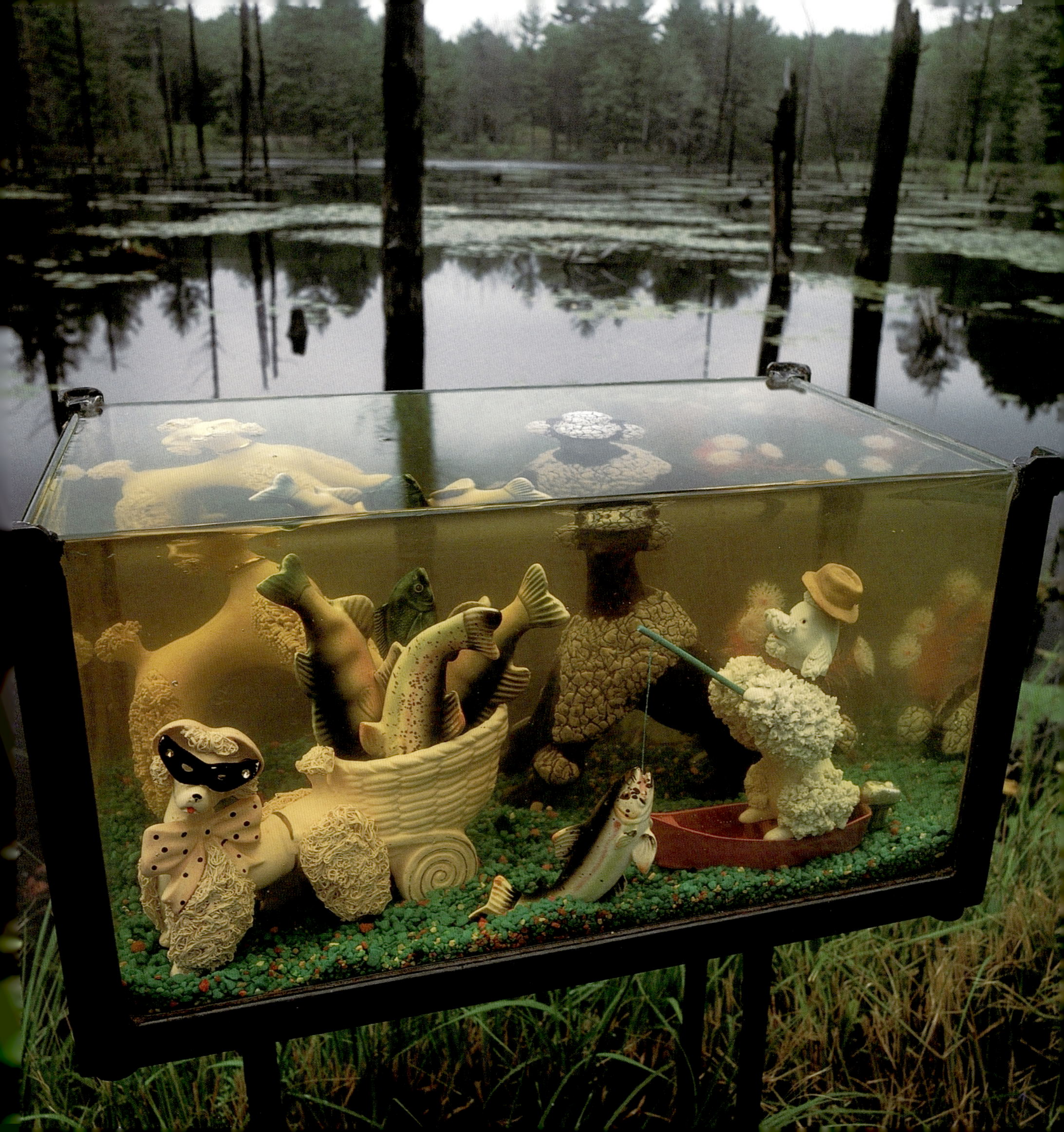

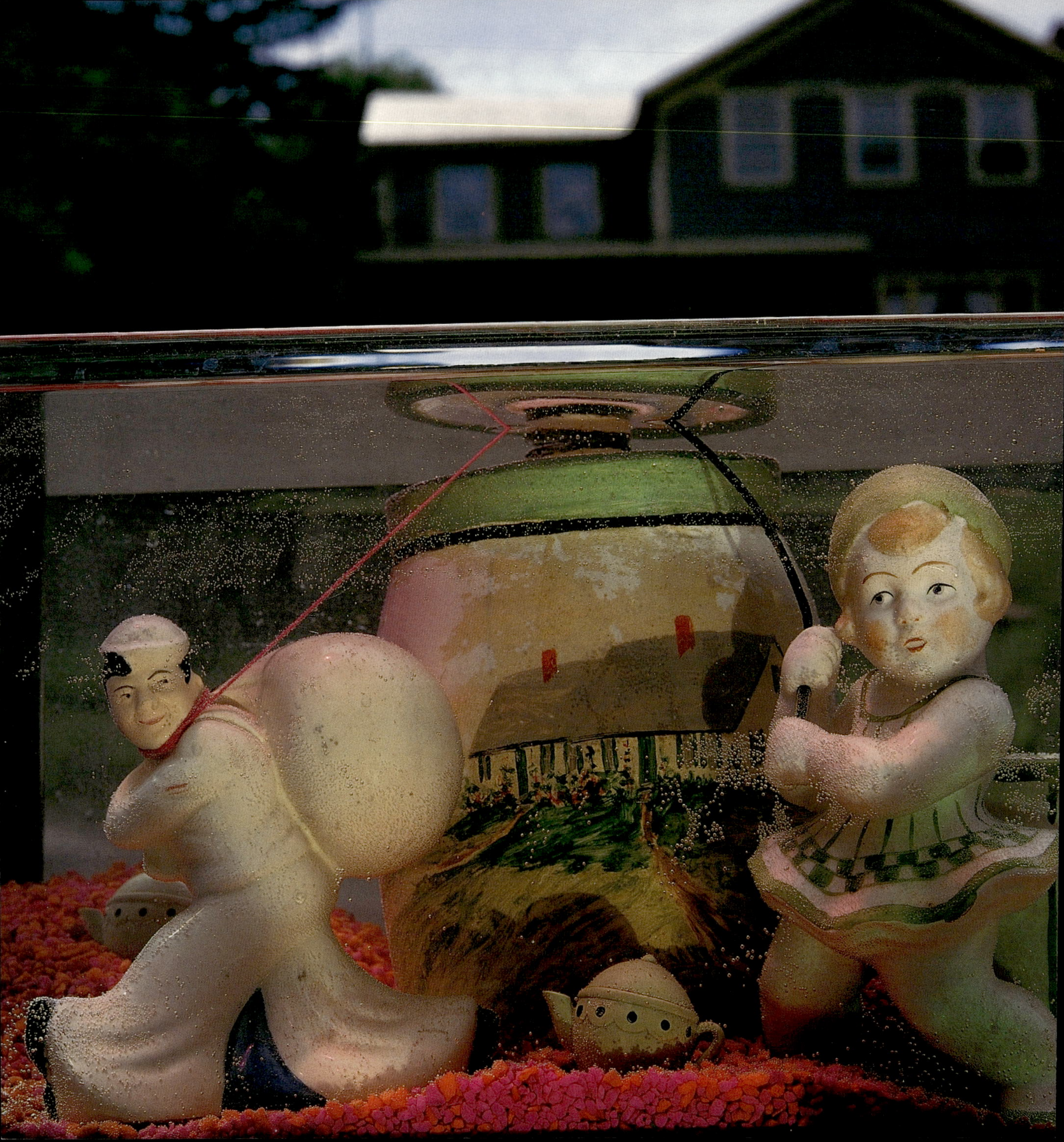

IV.
The Lures of Love

As the journey continues into its fourth movement, the fish guide explains to the fisherman the many aspects of love—romantic, domestic, jealous, and sublime—and how it is the passionate energy of desire that breaks down the artificial boundaries between humans and the natural world.

A fine and frothy day
Upon a timeless strand
A goddess was blown by humid winds
Onward to the land.

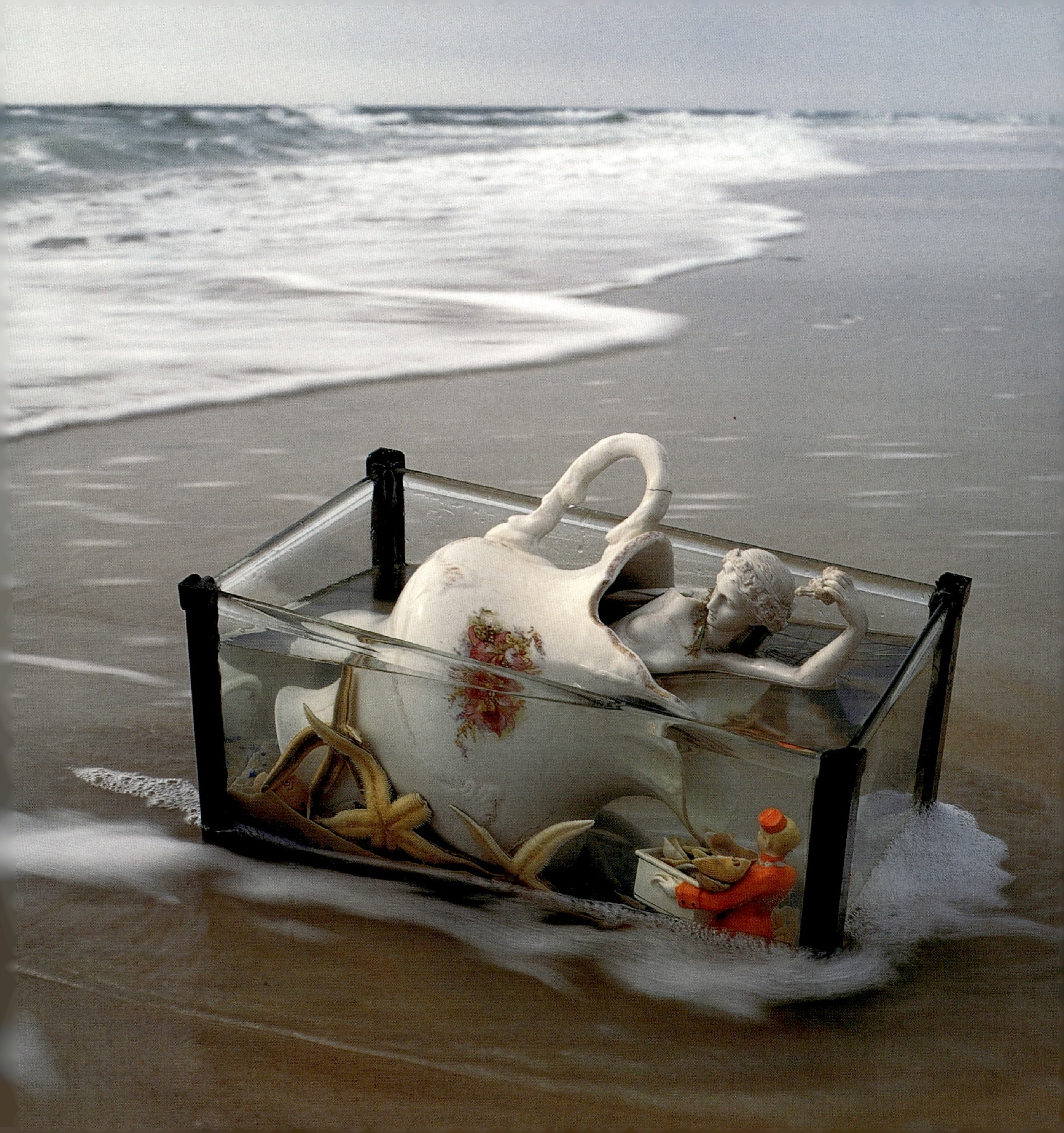

A golden carp whispered
Bits of ancient lore:
Earthly seductions to
Bring her men by the score.

84)

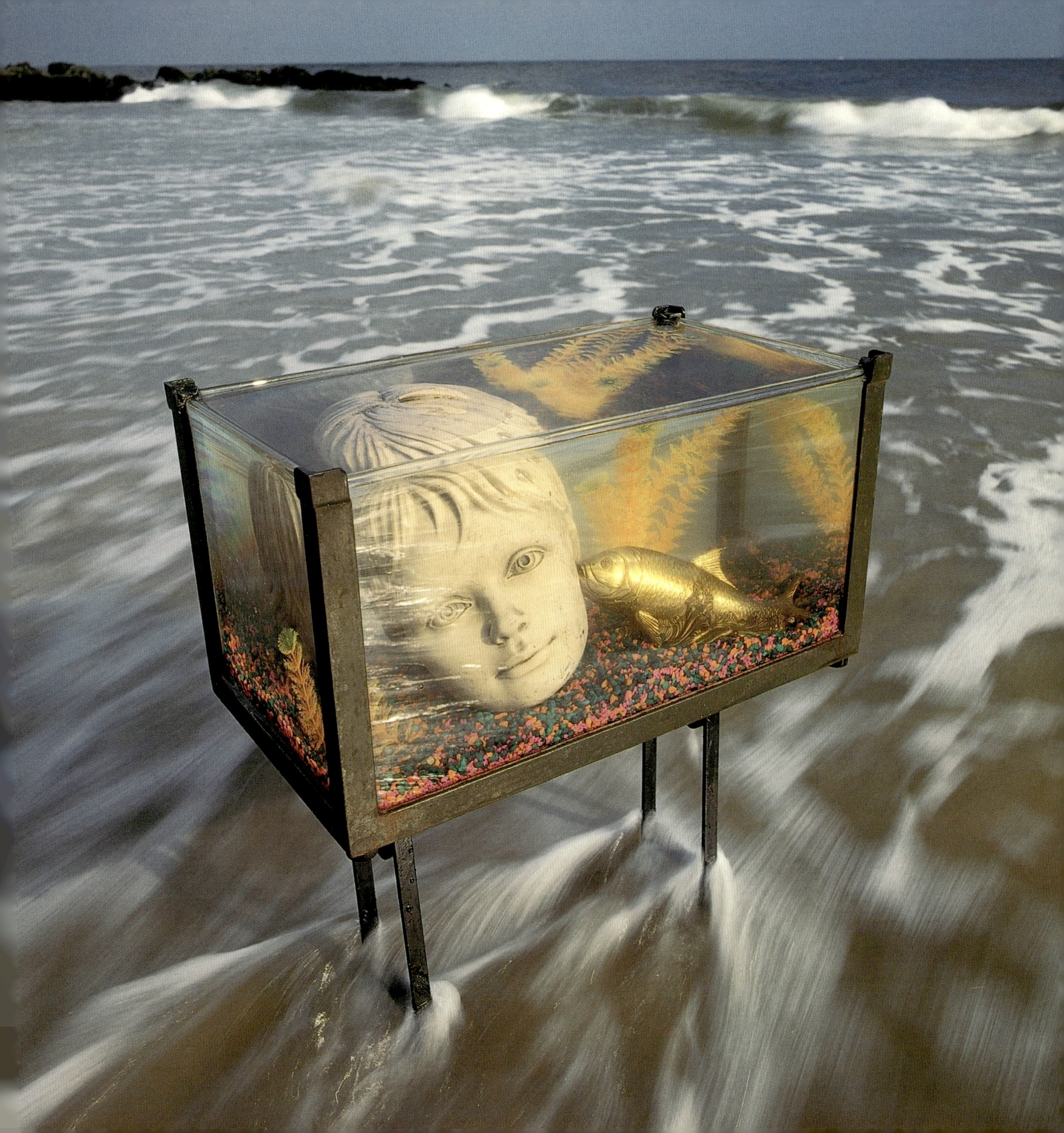

Bare-breasted beauties frolicking on a rocky shore
Drive men mad with bubbling excitement never felt before.

86]

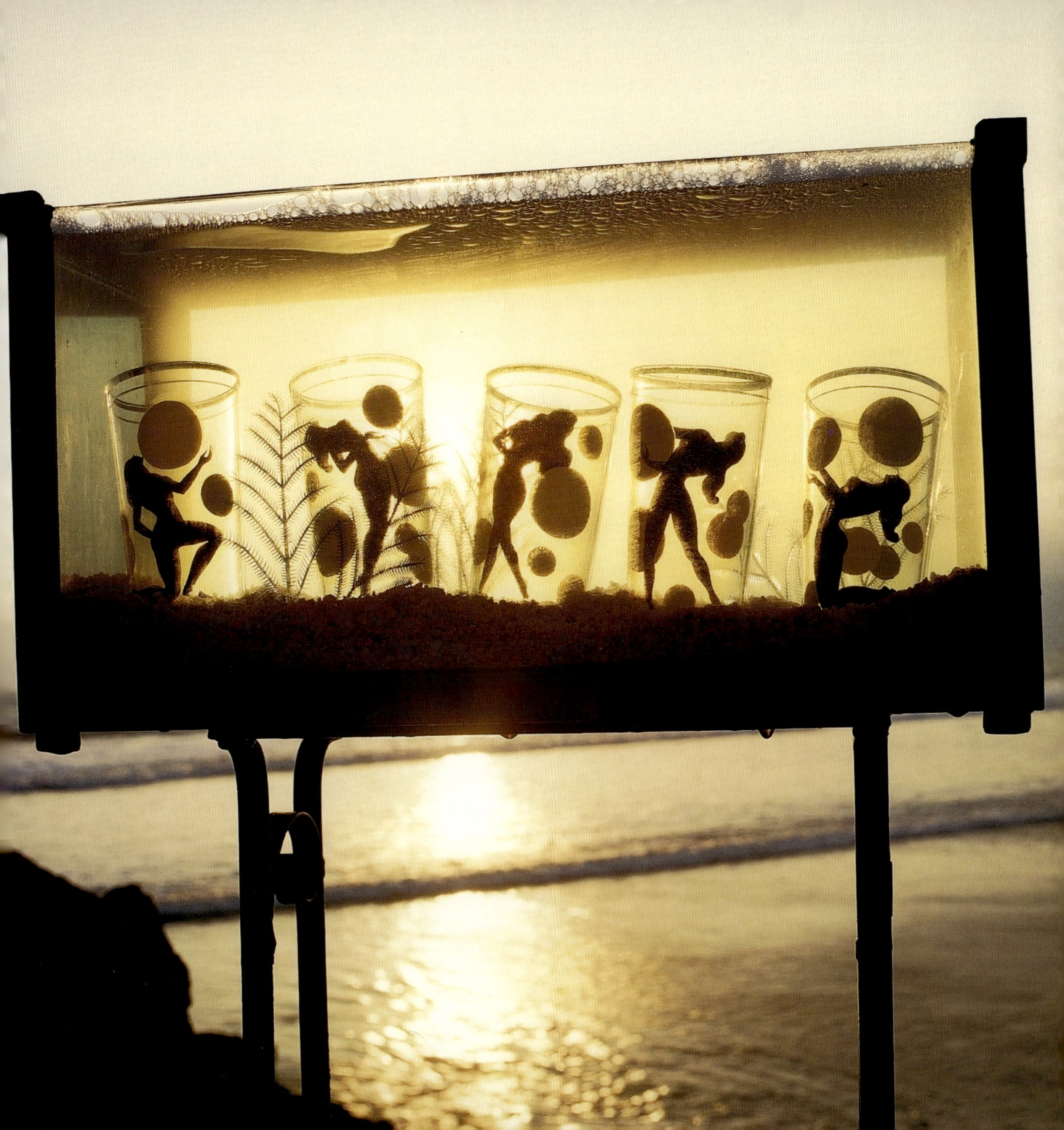

Love-besotted couples drift beyond us
To rapturous islands they alone have found.
Time's river will part and slow for them,
And for a while flow around.

88)

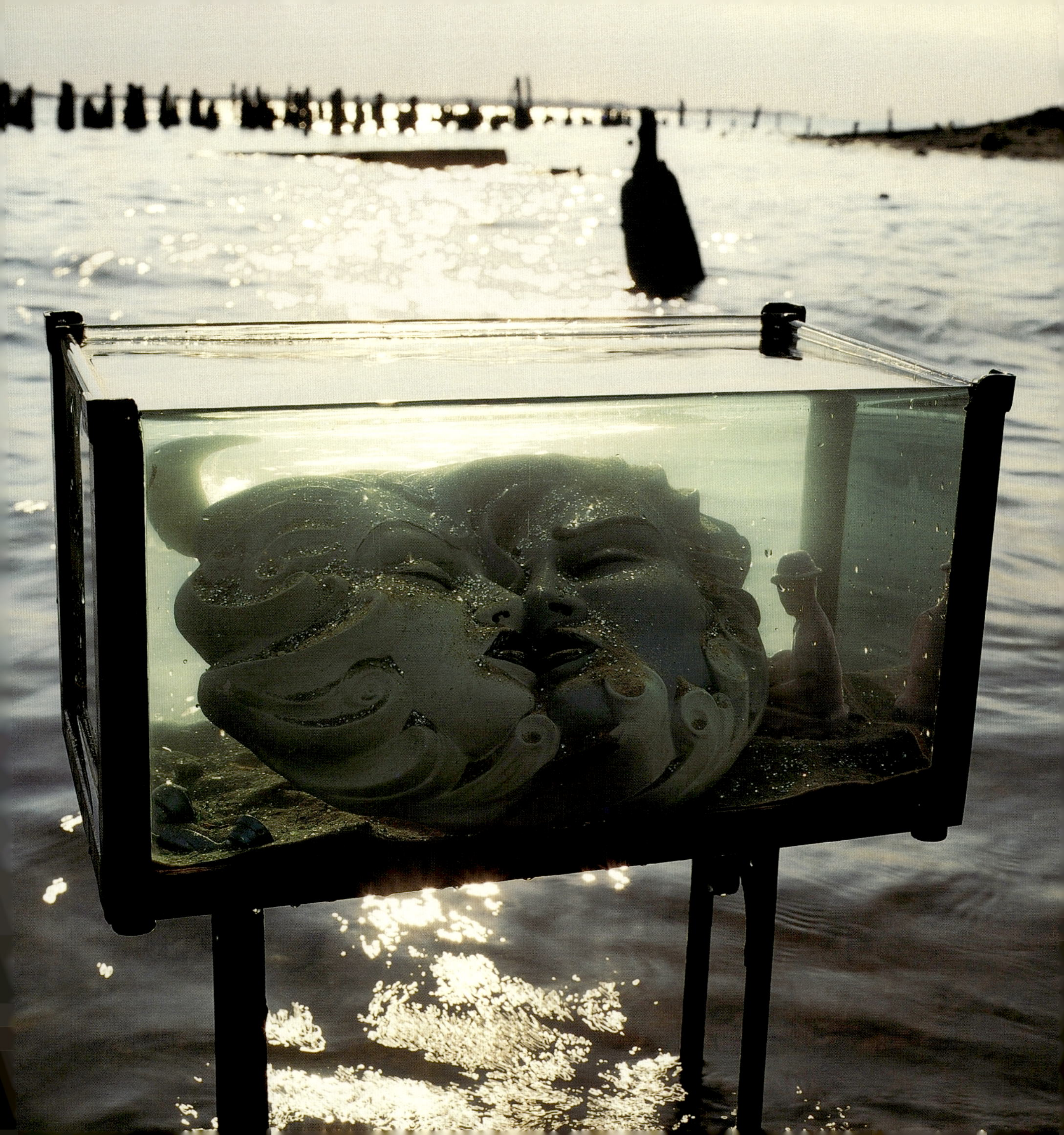

Slipping like a fish
Through dark and narrow streams,
Nocturnal desires rise
And trouble our dreams.

90)

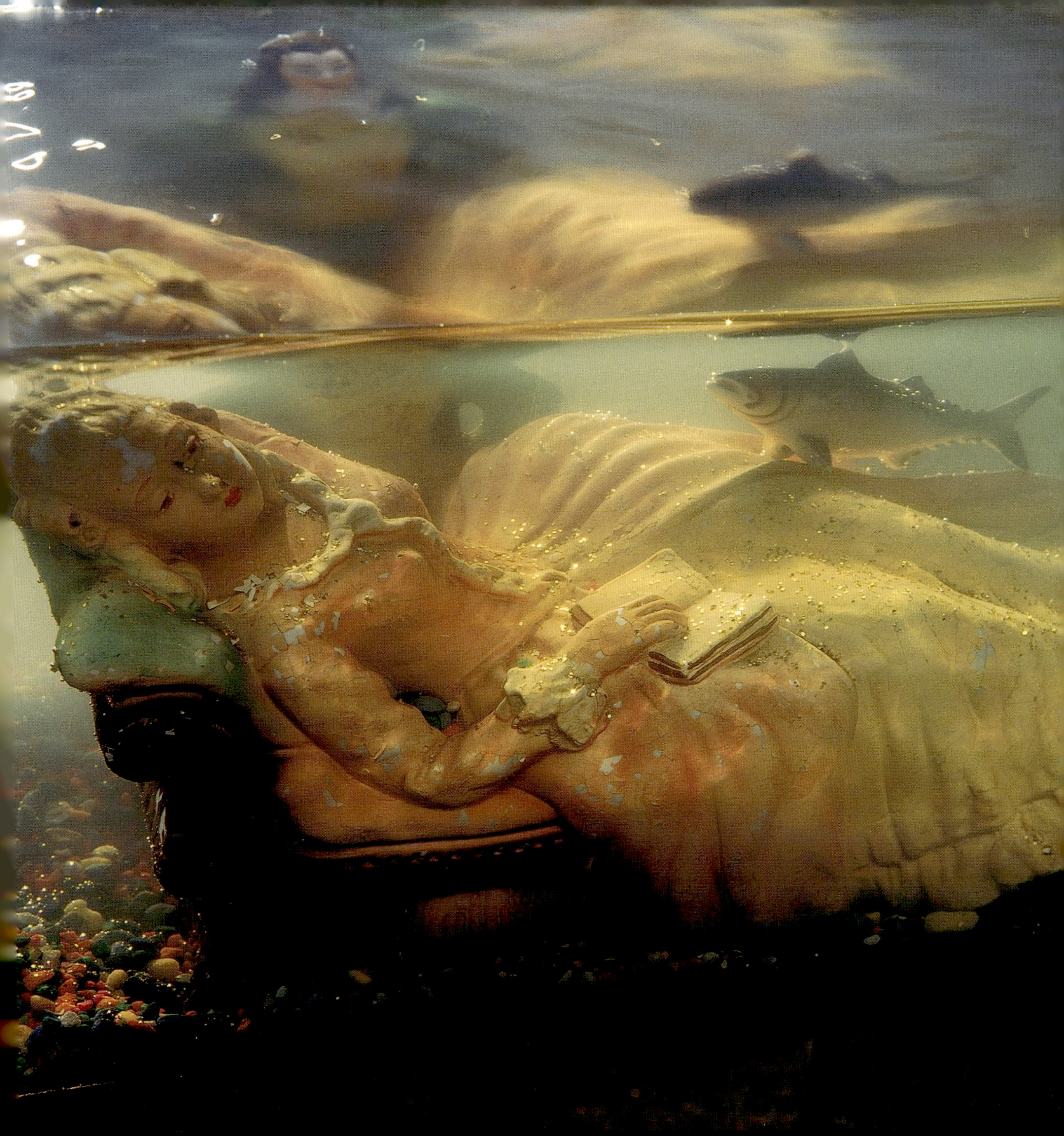

But the gentle currents also bring
Secret pleasures and oneiric bliss
To an aging courtesan
Dreaming of a kiss.

92]

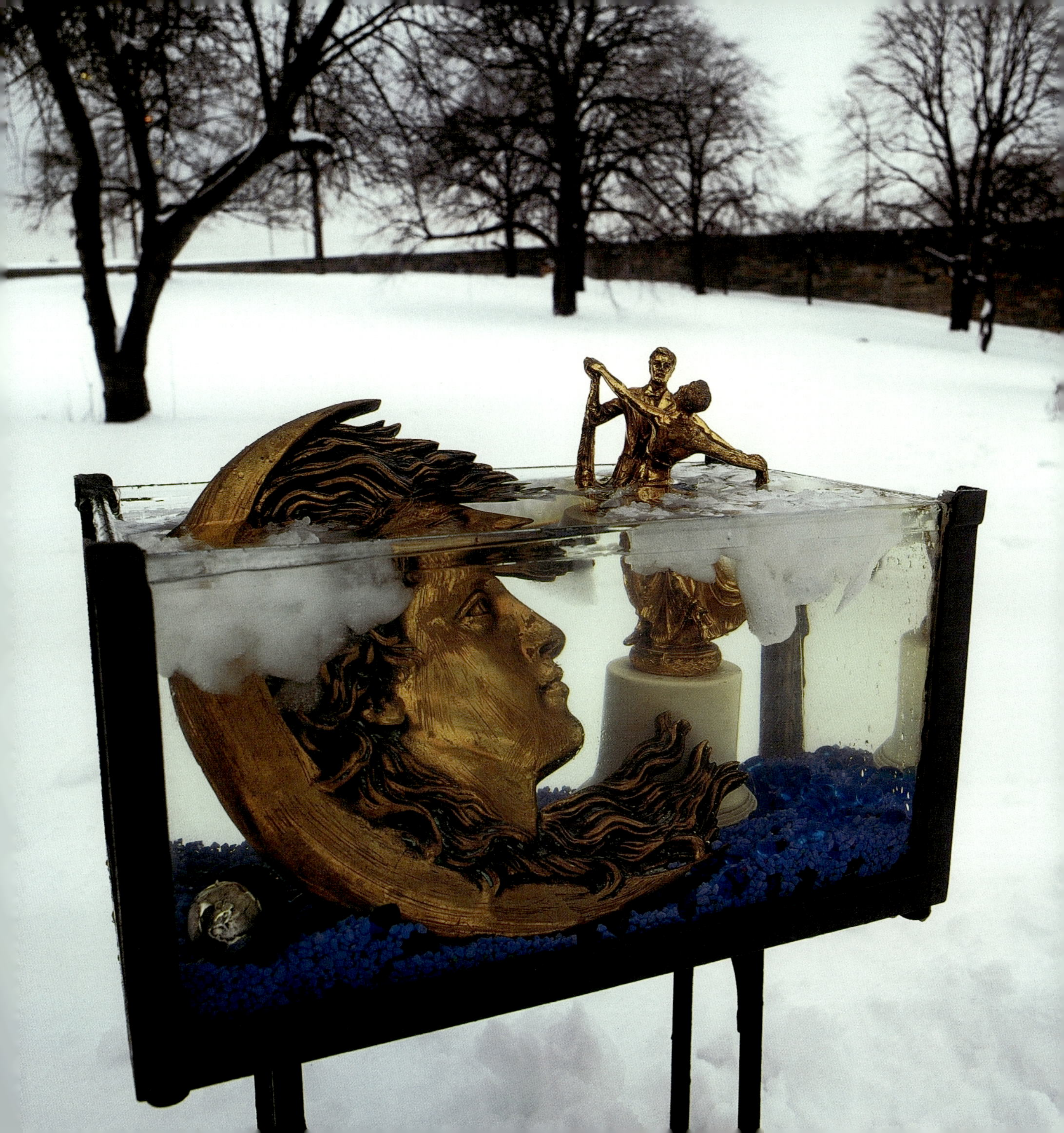

The vernal joy betides the genius
Who would surely rather dream
Than be enlisted to cogitate
For the military research team.

94)

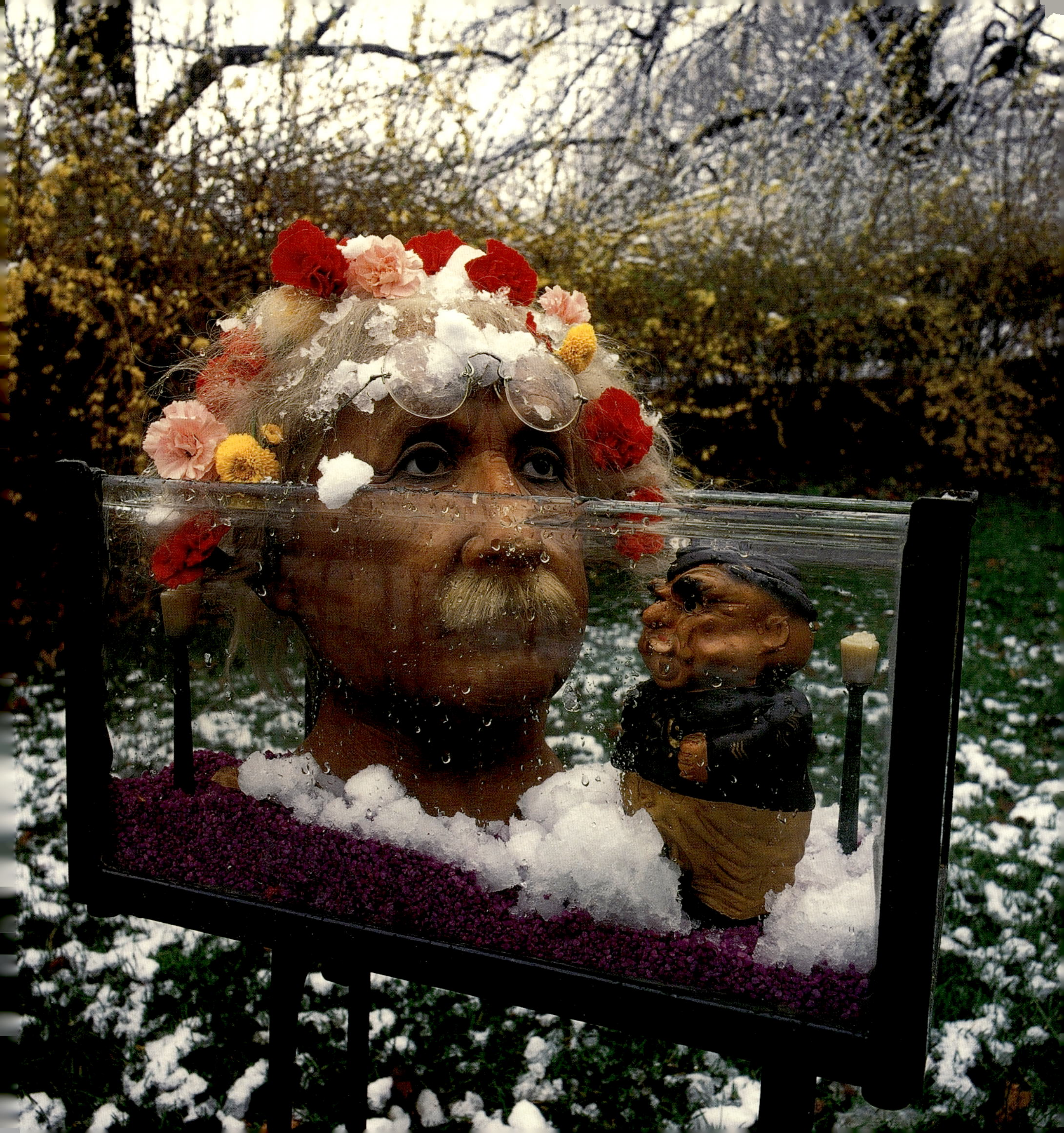

The American Grizzly,
Driven mad with desires,
Scares the girl away
With the screeching of his tires.

96)

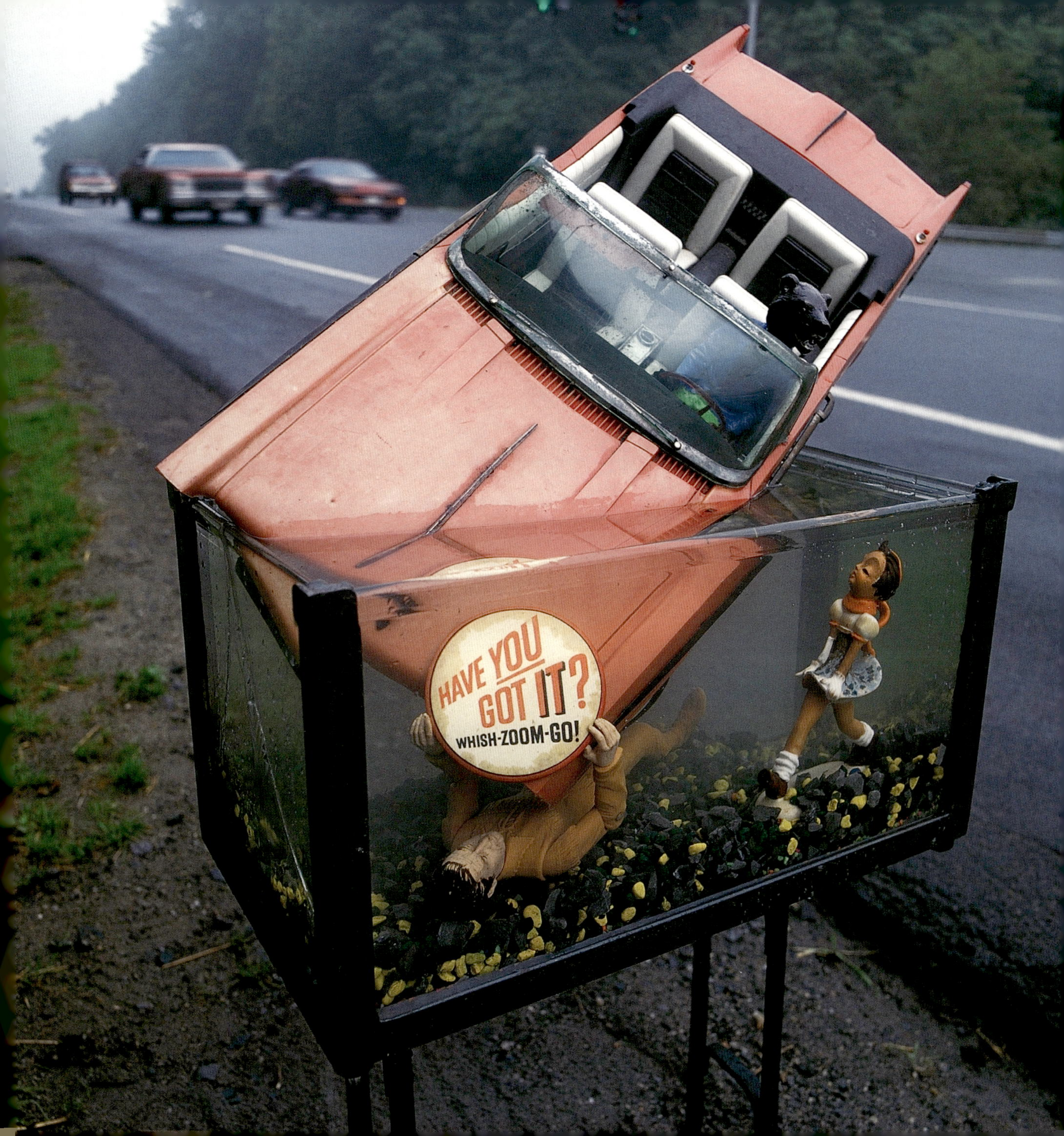

HAVE YOU GOT IT?
WHISH-ZOOM-GO!

Mr. Grimes is closely watched
By his shrewish wife from hell.
Could we read his fantasies,
We'd see his neighbor Nell.

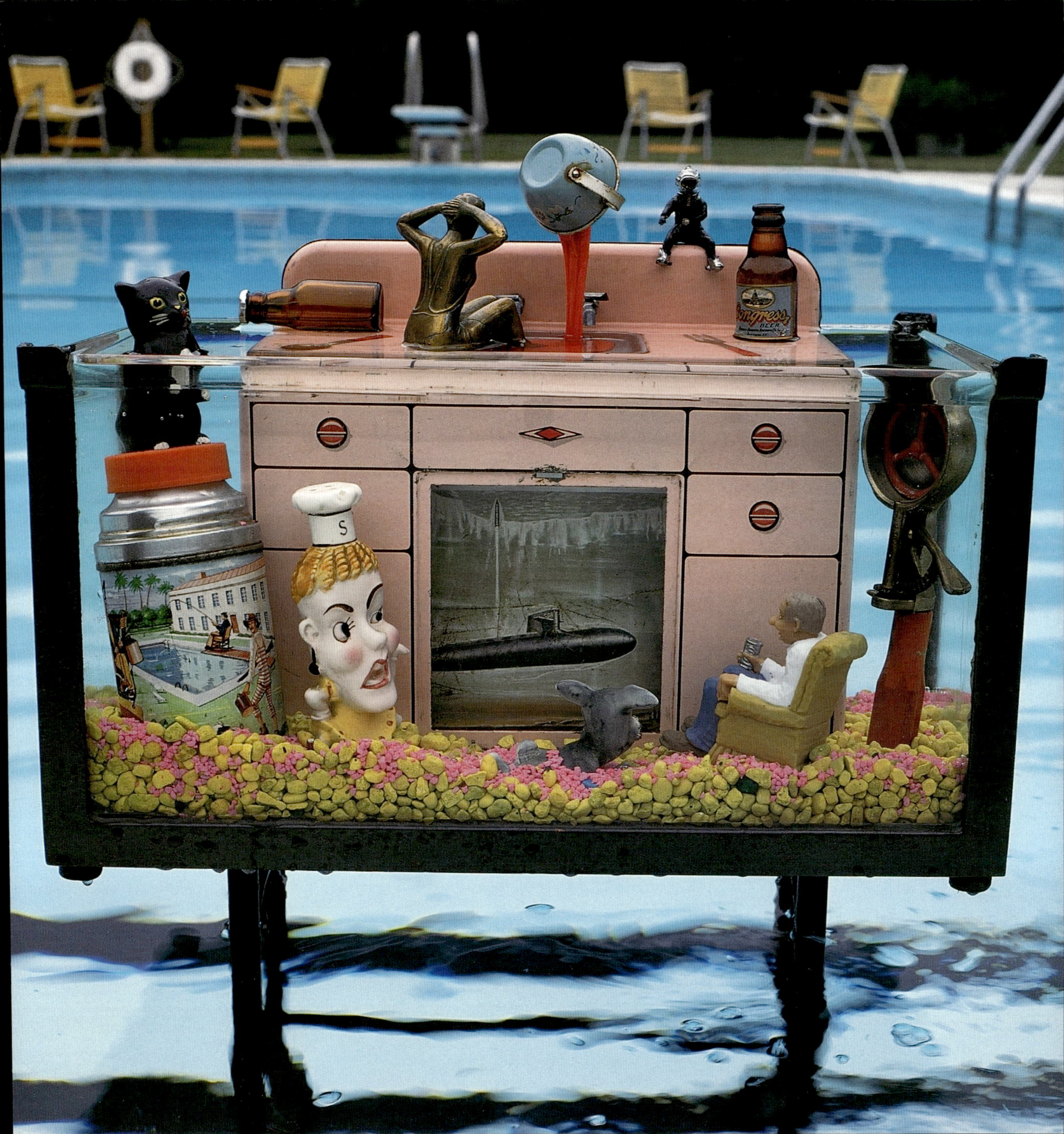

Like a spawning fish
Flushed bright and smart,
The Prince of Atlantis
Romances his tropical sweetheart.

100)

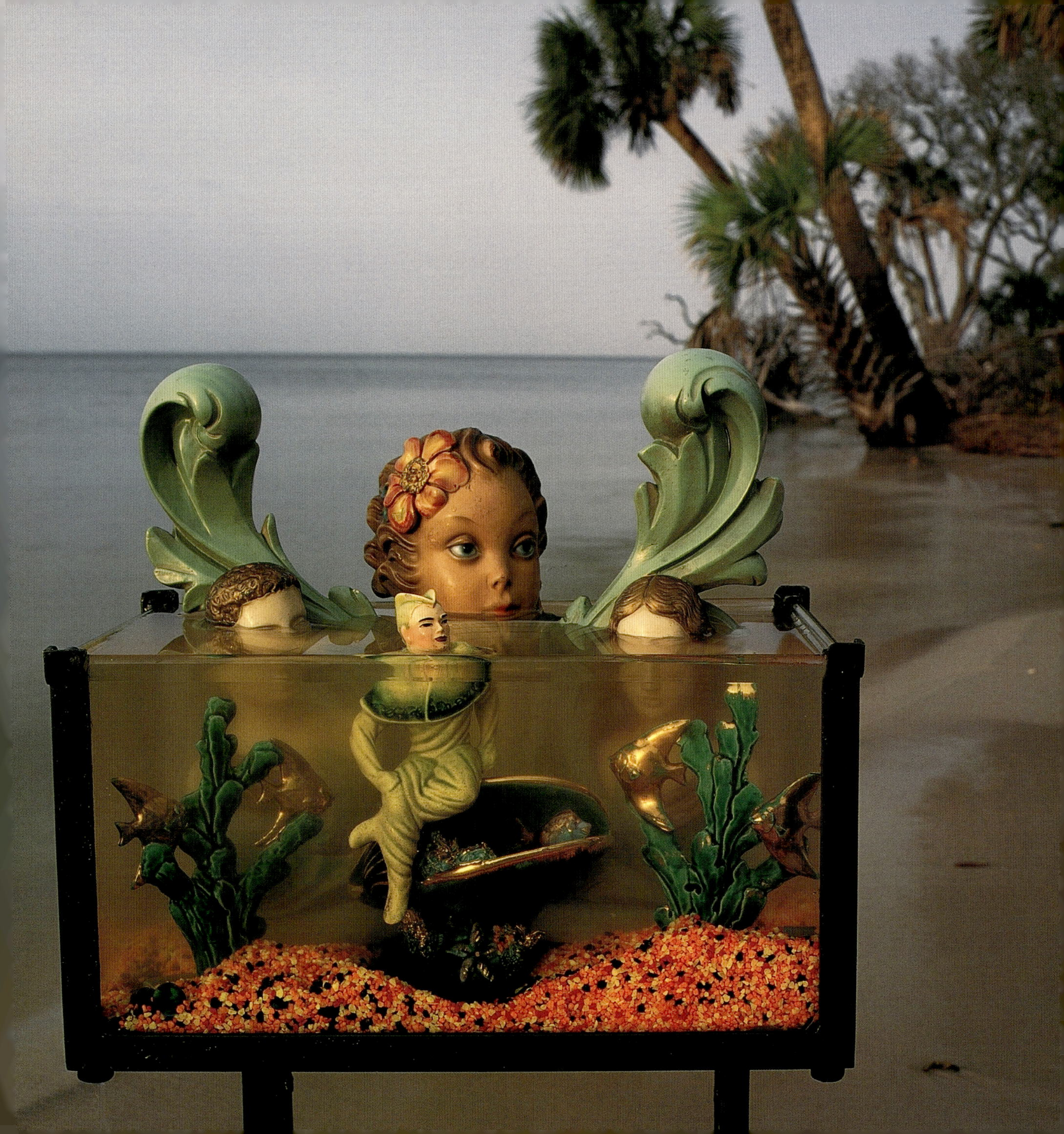

Jealous suitors still preen and fret,
Crying and praying as to whether they'll get
A flowery tryst with that most heavenly and wet
Swan maiden the world has seen yet.

102)

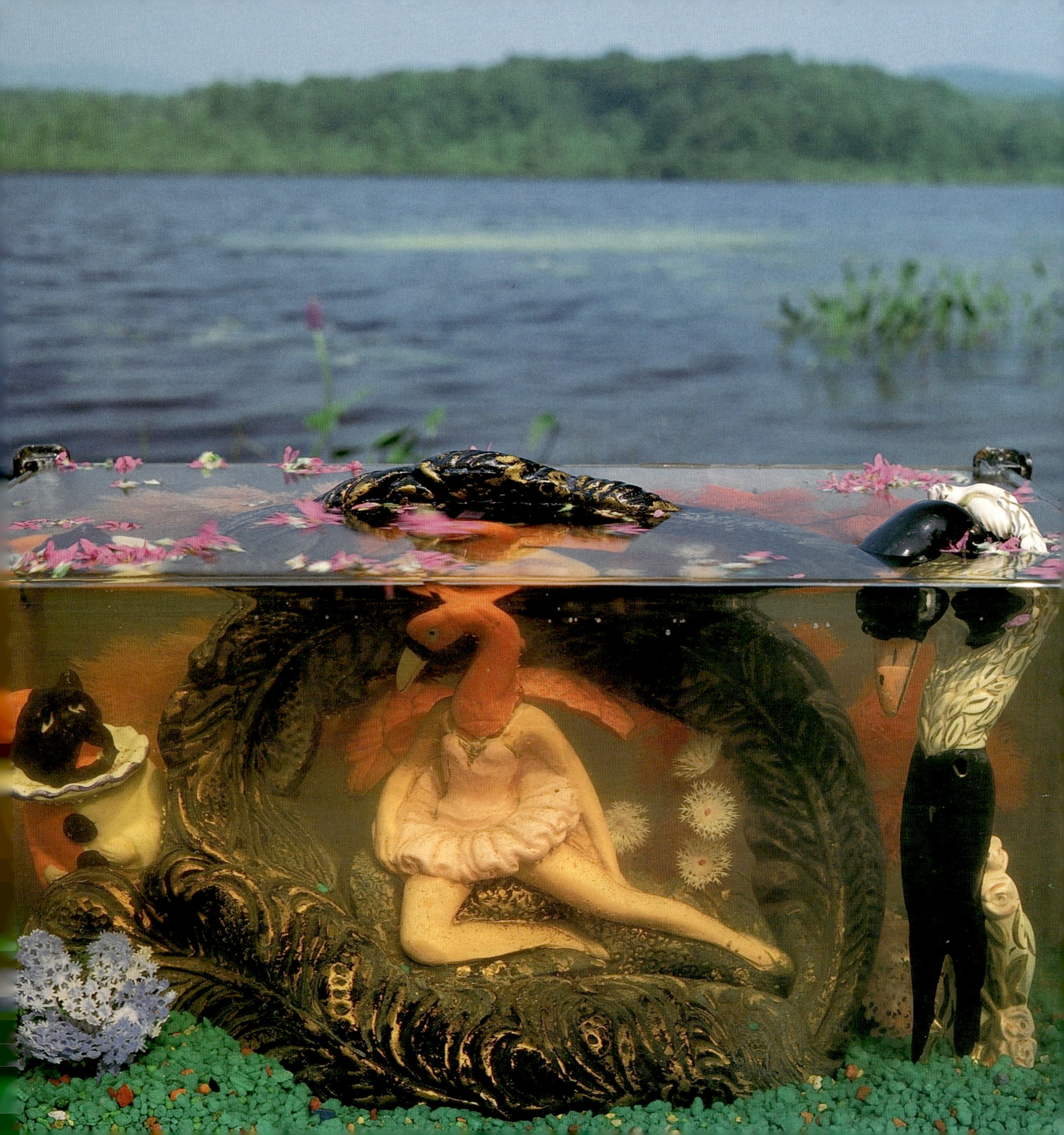

In quiet glades close by the waters
Flocks of young lovers pet and caress
The pliable mates they've just so impressed.

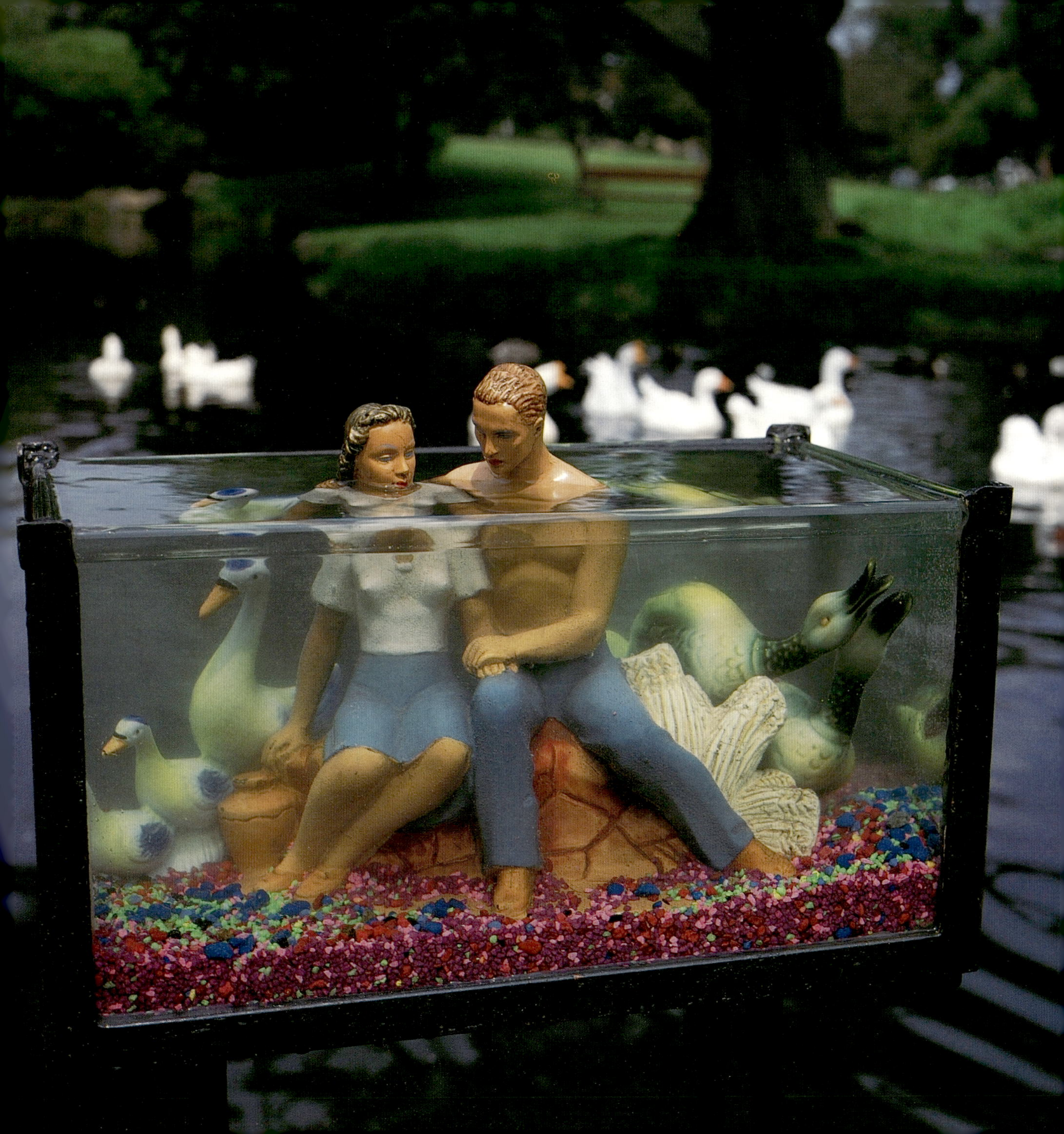

Howls echo over the hills
As the lone wolf beckons a friend;
In this wide-open country,
Solitude may in fact be his end.

106)

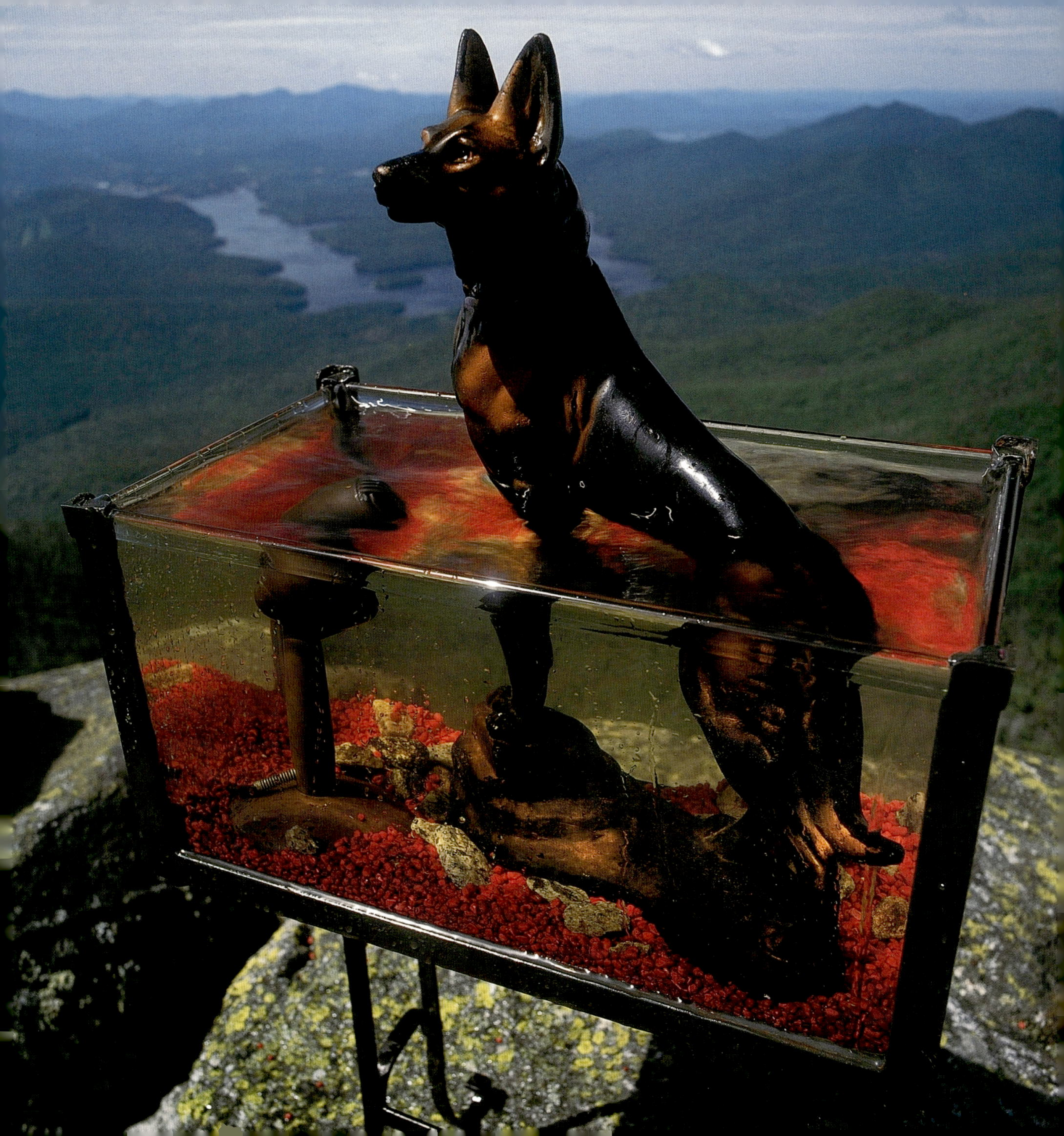

But the harvest songs ring
Down in the fields,
Where people are happy
With what the earth yields.

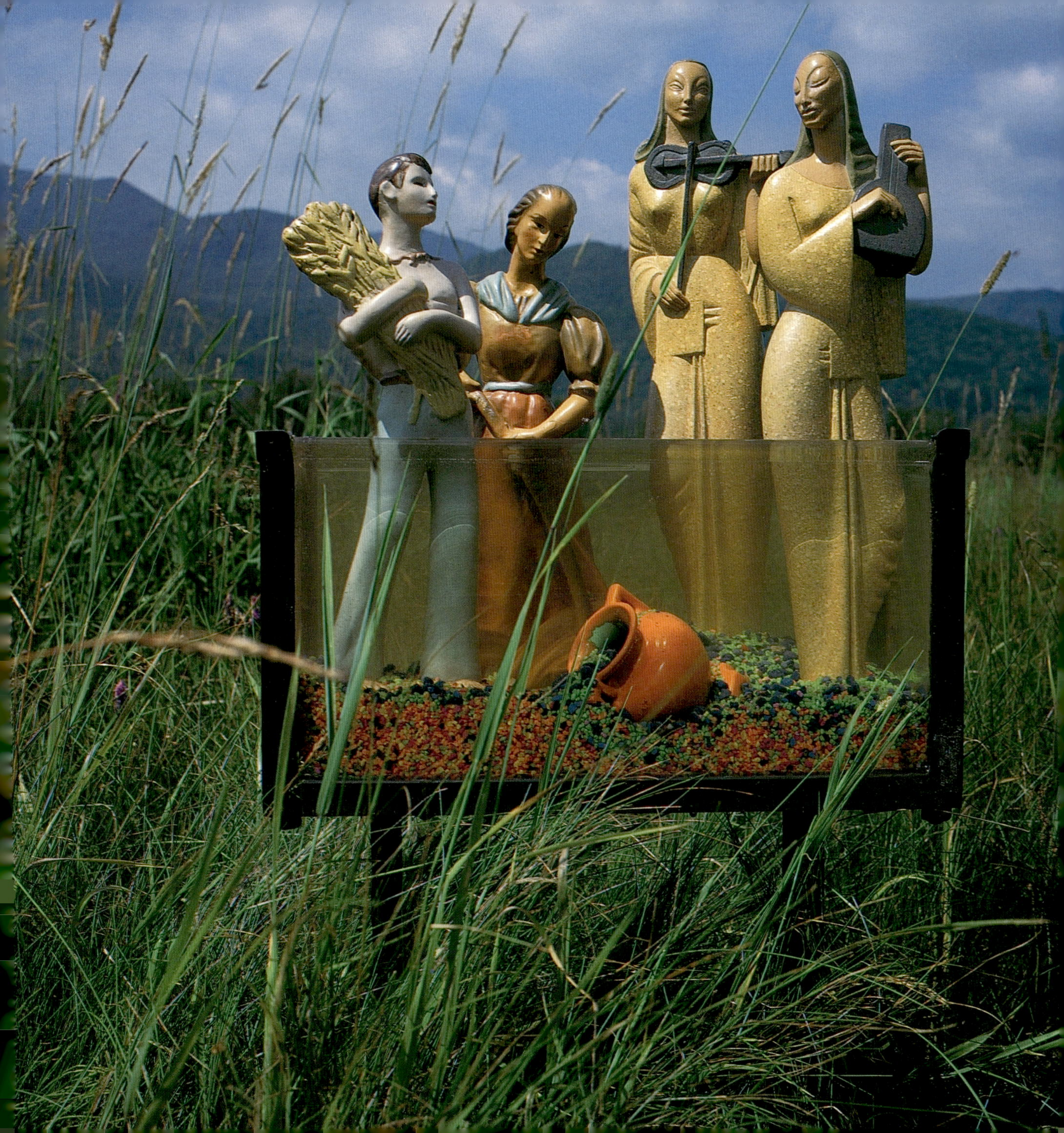

Hark to the medley
Of the insects' gentle hum:
Their cumulative music
Overwhelms our small sum.

110)

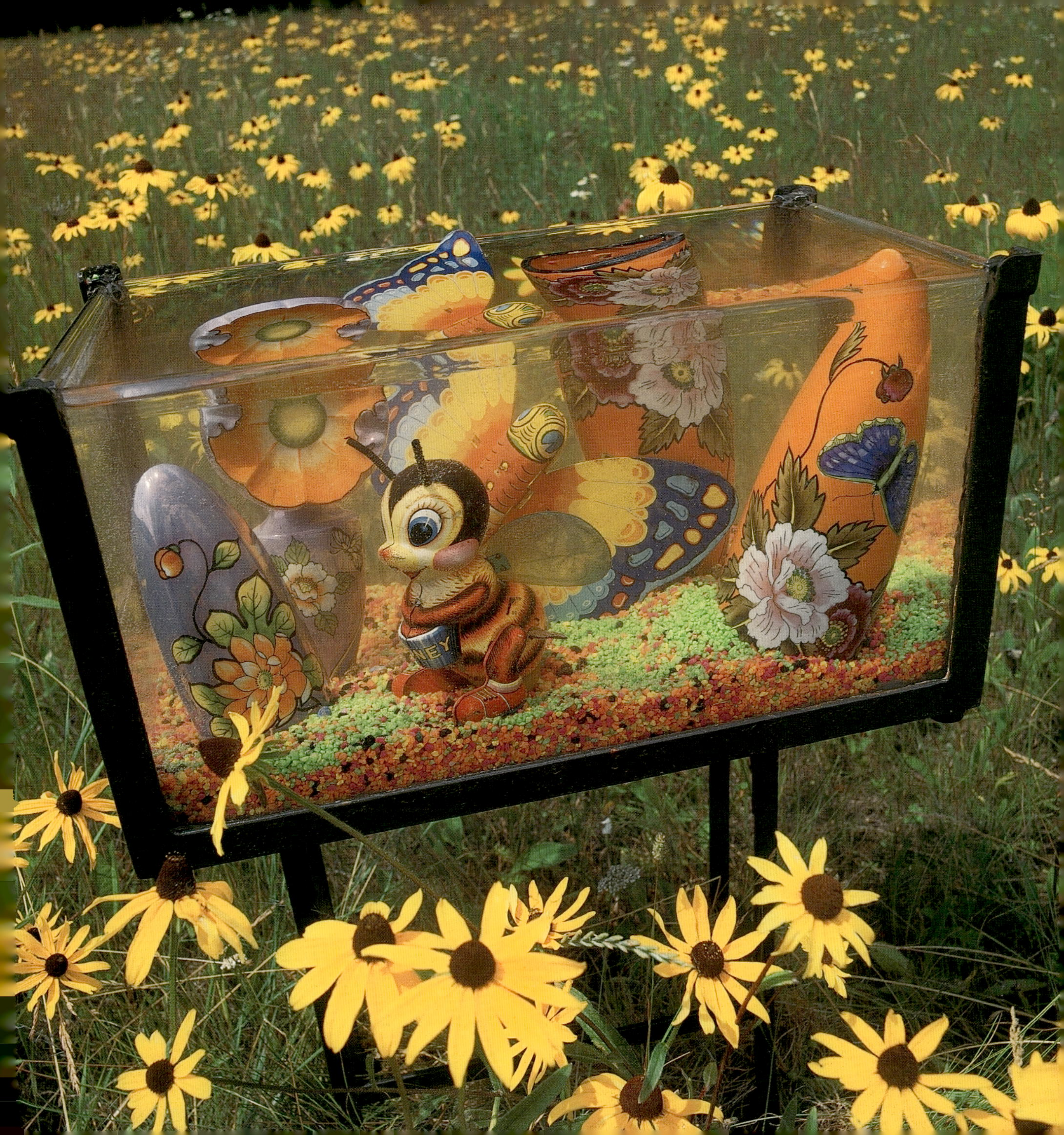

The jungle of your soul,
Chaotic and steamy,
Will sing with the summer
So heated and dreamy.

112)

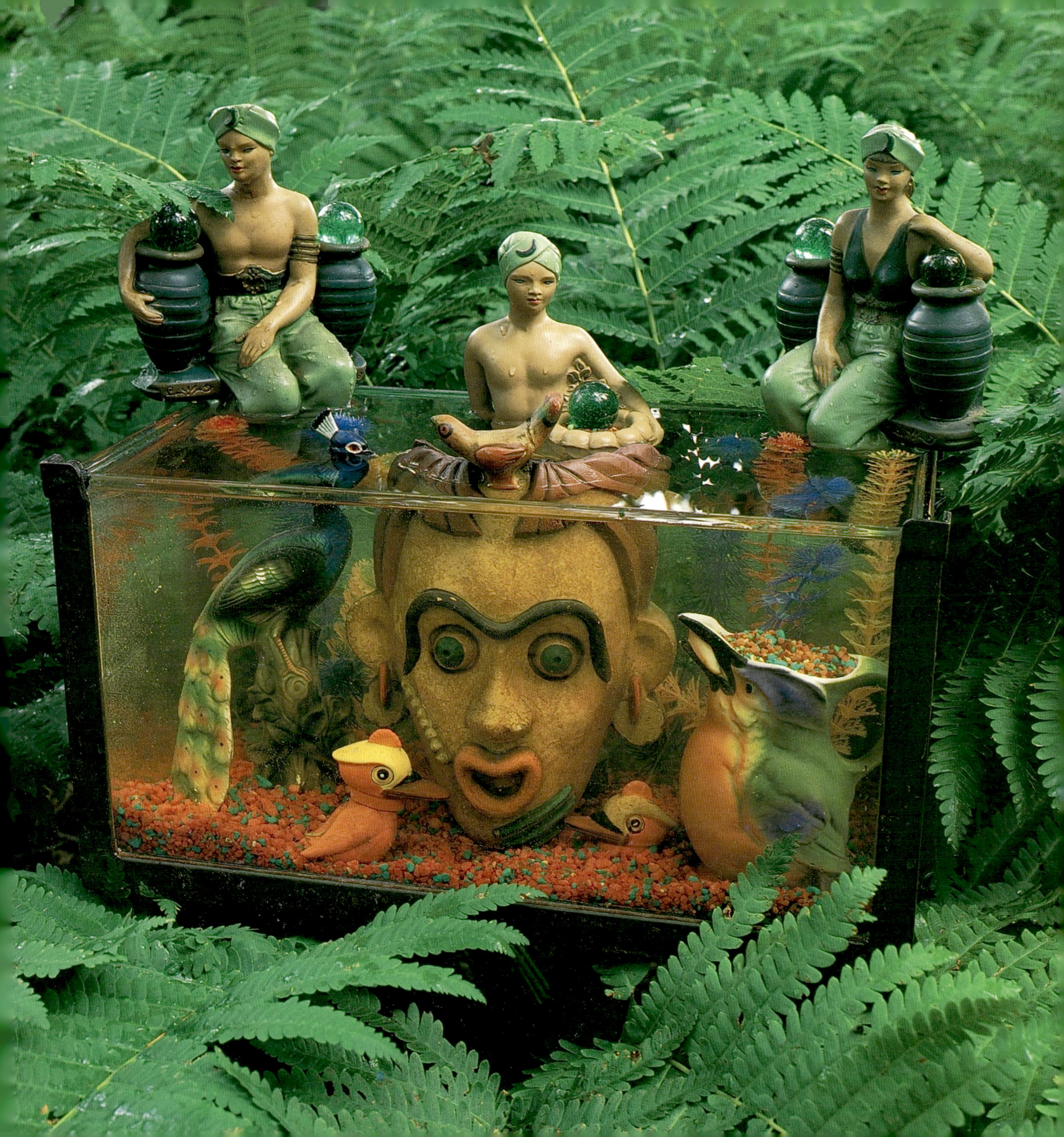

Abandon your worries!
Abandon your reason!
Join with the revelers
And dance to the season.

114)

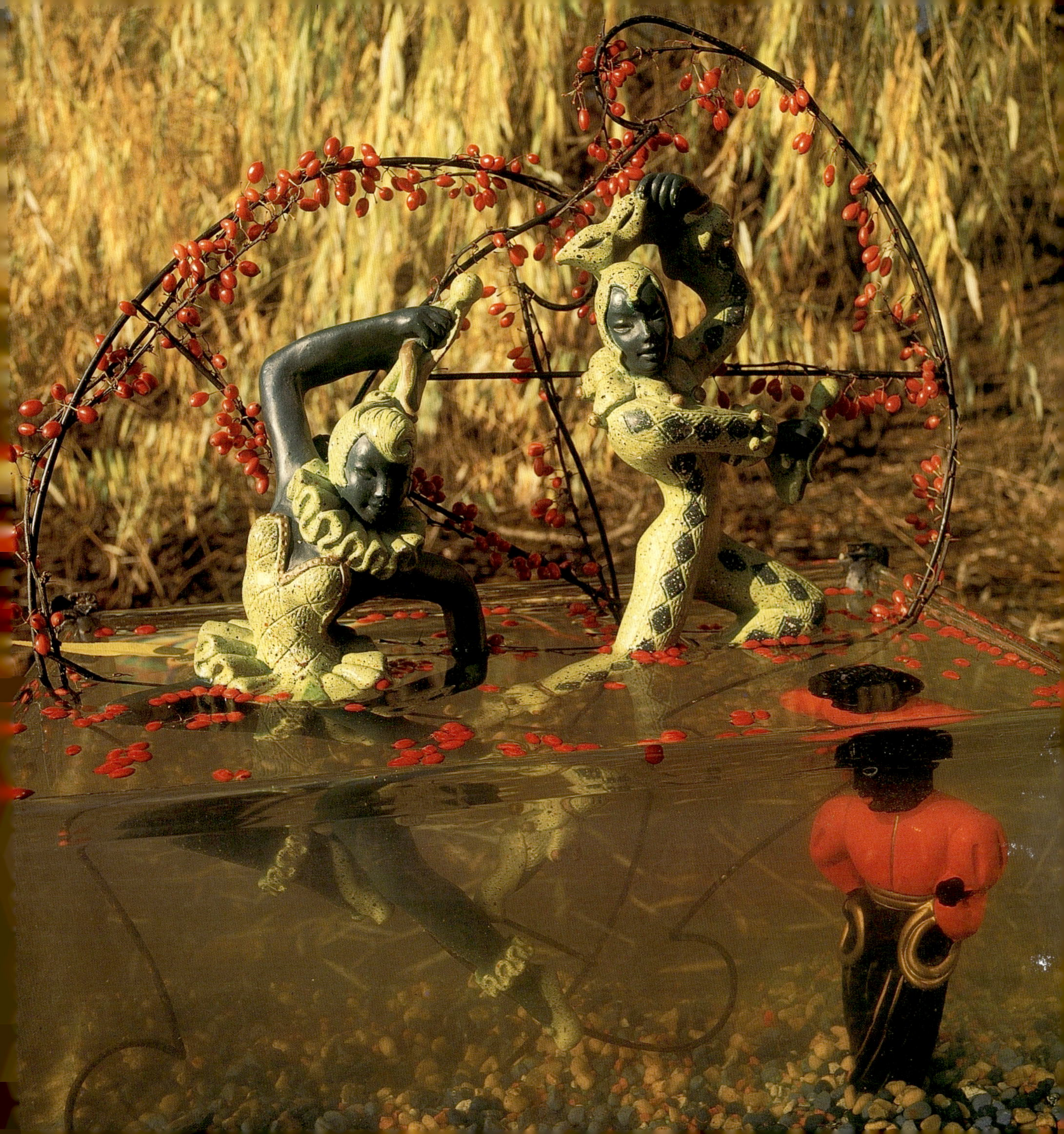

Dance for the chaos,
Dance for the order;
Feel jubilation
Here by the water.

This is only commencement.
With all that you've learned,
Go now and see
How the world can be turned.

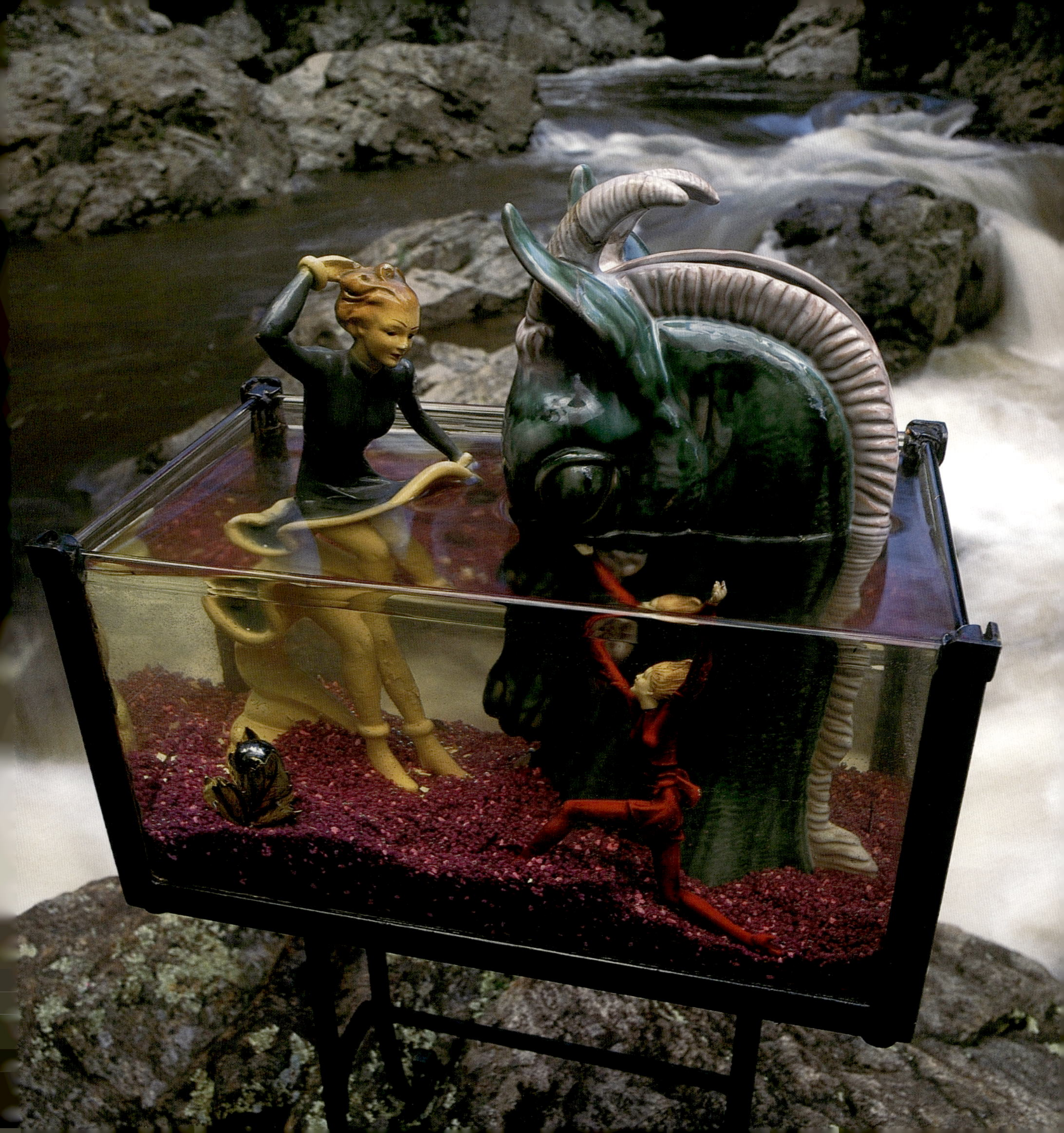

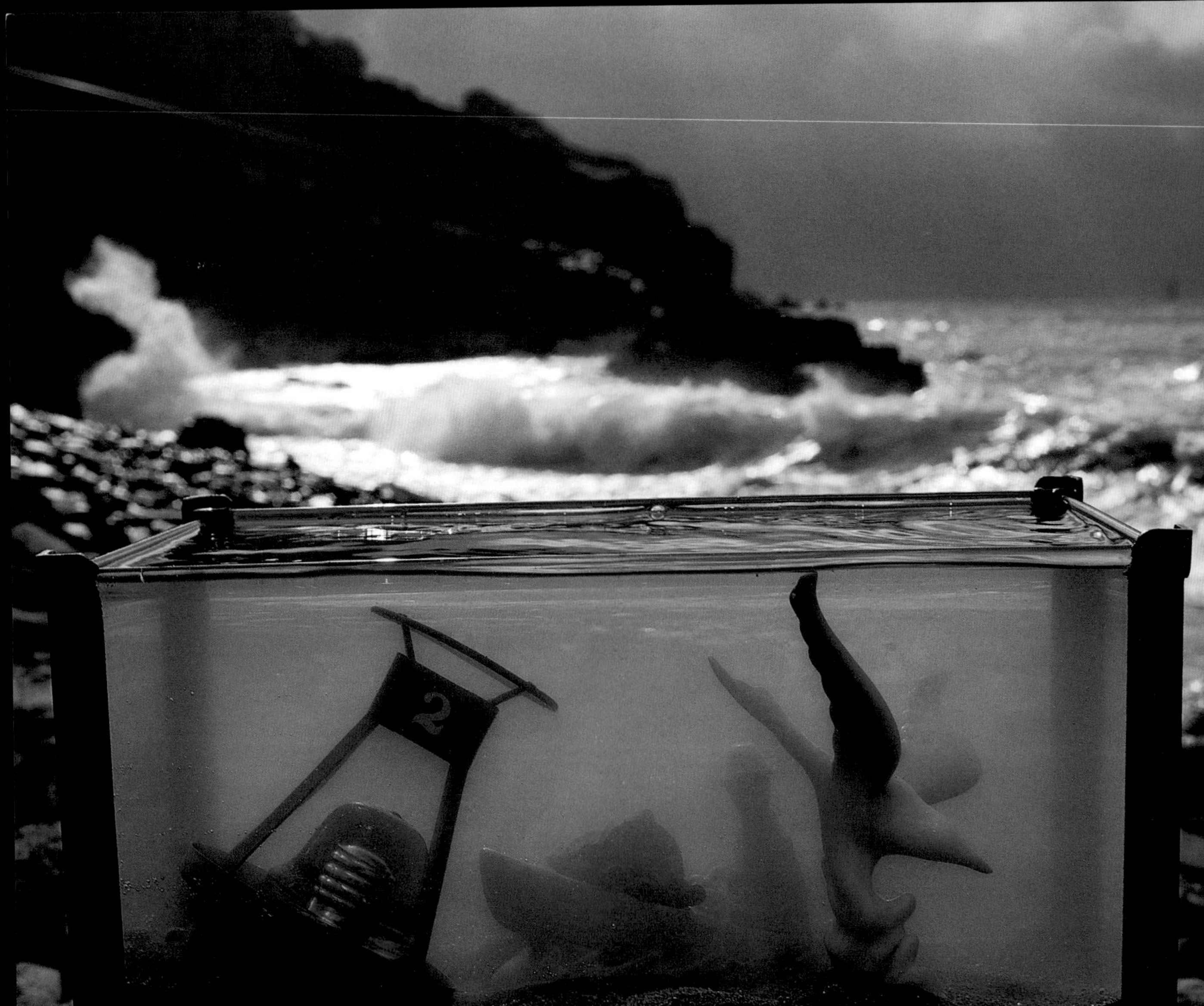

V.
Home

In this fifth and final movement, the fisherman takes
leave of his finny friend, eager to test out his newly acquired
pescatorial skills. Upon his return he finds the natural order
in chaos. He realizes he must become a caretaker of the
earthly realm if he, and his guide, are to survive in it—their
fate is bound together in one indissoluble grasp.

The next day he set sail,
Illuminated and wiser,
Bound for home changed
By the teachings of his sage adviser.

120)

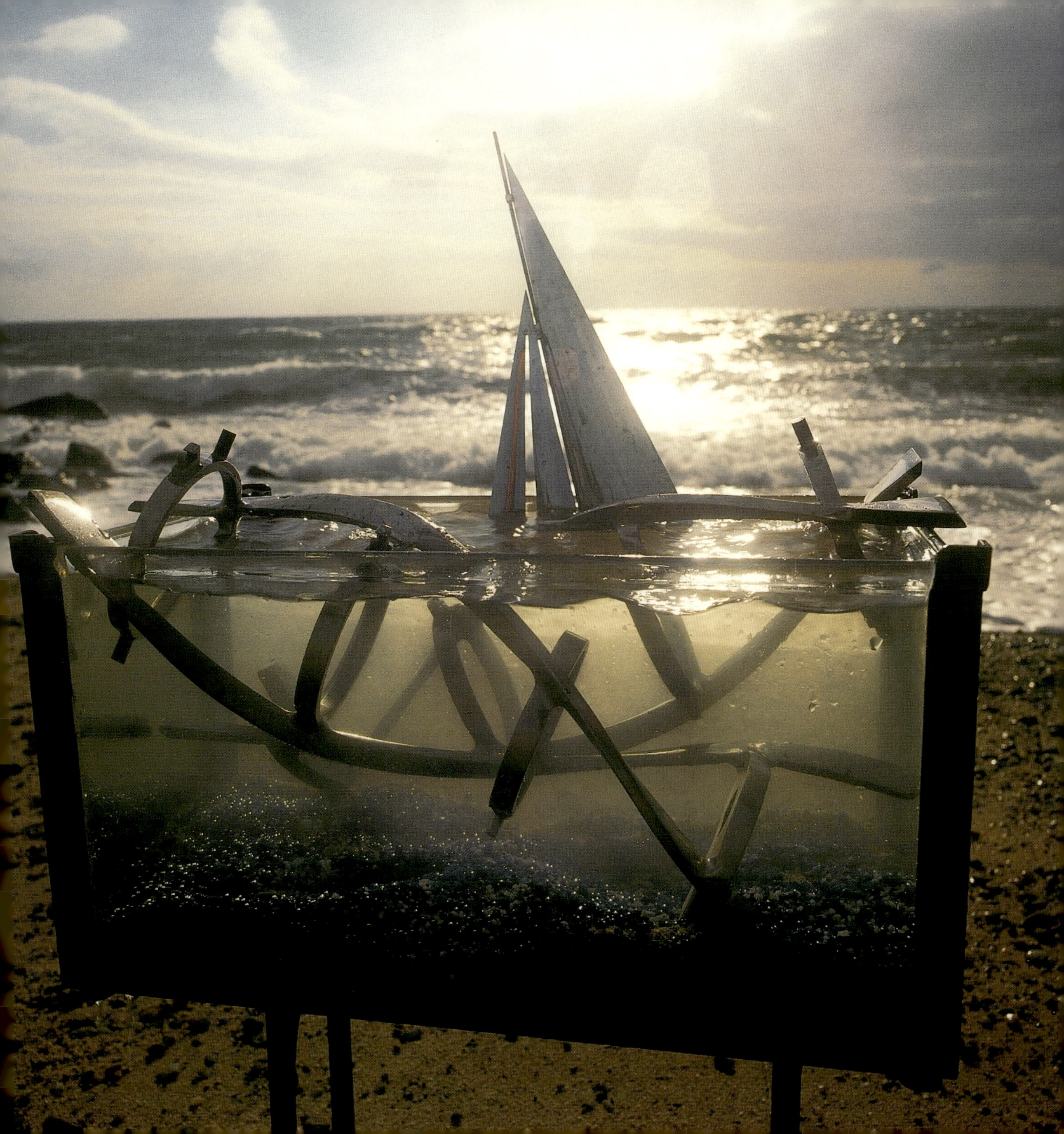

Drifting by the home of the
Old man who times the tide,
He felt the ineluctable
Pull of gravity inside.

122)

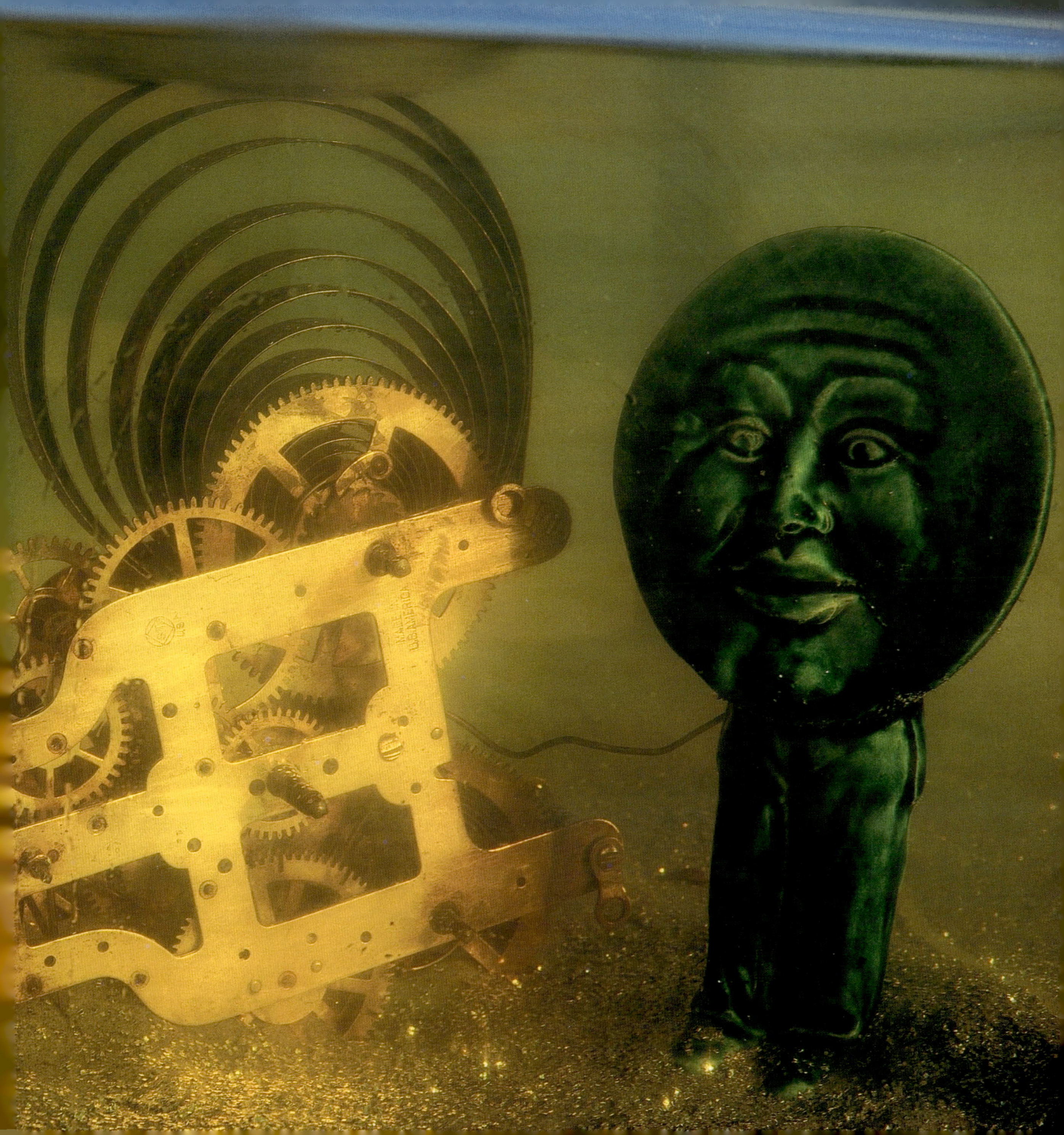

Our Lady of the Conch Shell
Blessed the boats at sea
From the shrine where she dwells
So they'd fish successfully.

124)

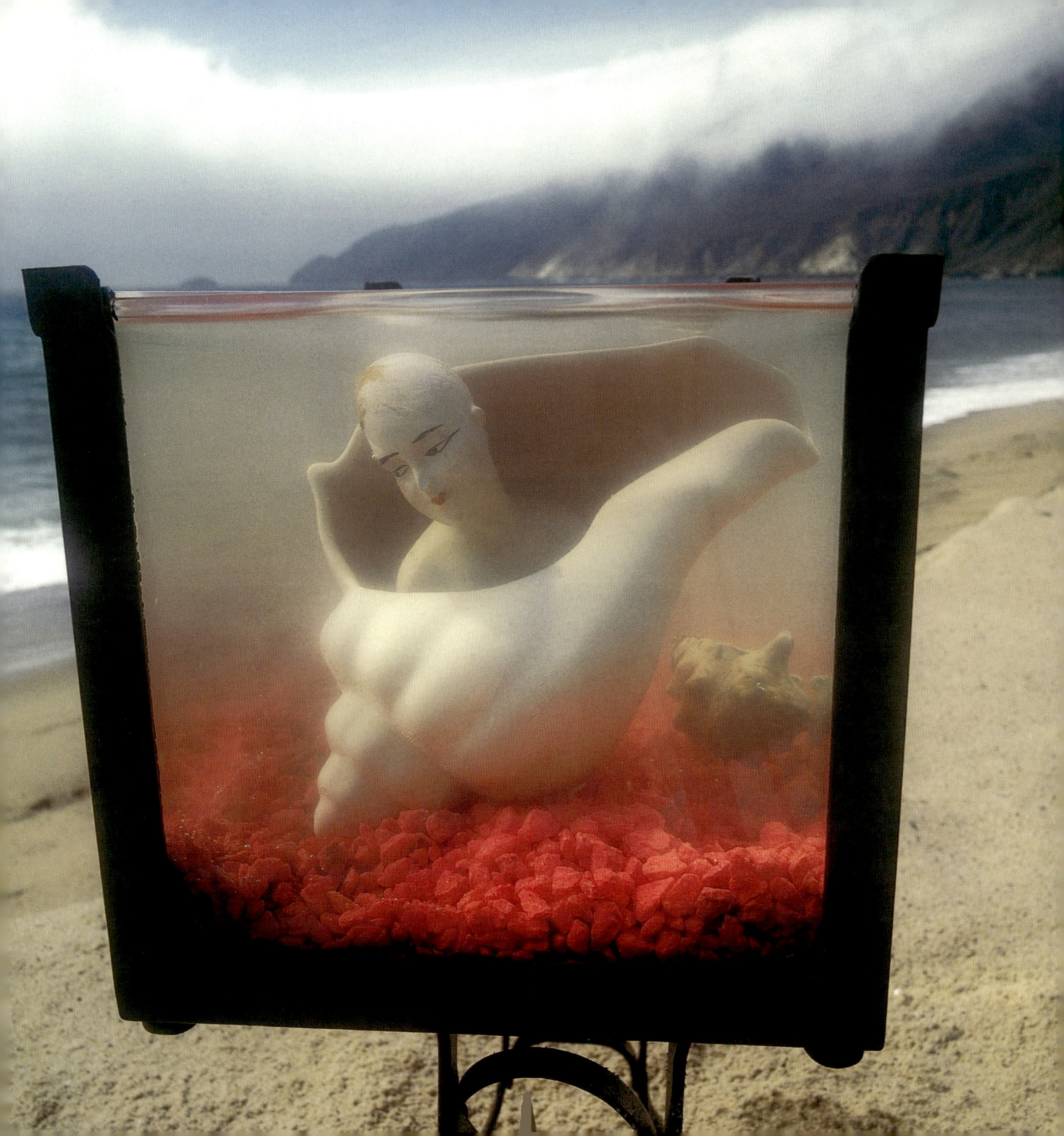

But the tides brought no fruit from the sea.
No fish would rise for bait or flies;
The ocean seemed sick and ailing permanently.

The malady was quite severe—
A chronic case, so it appeared,
Desperately needing emergency care.

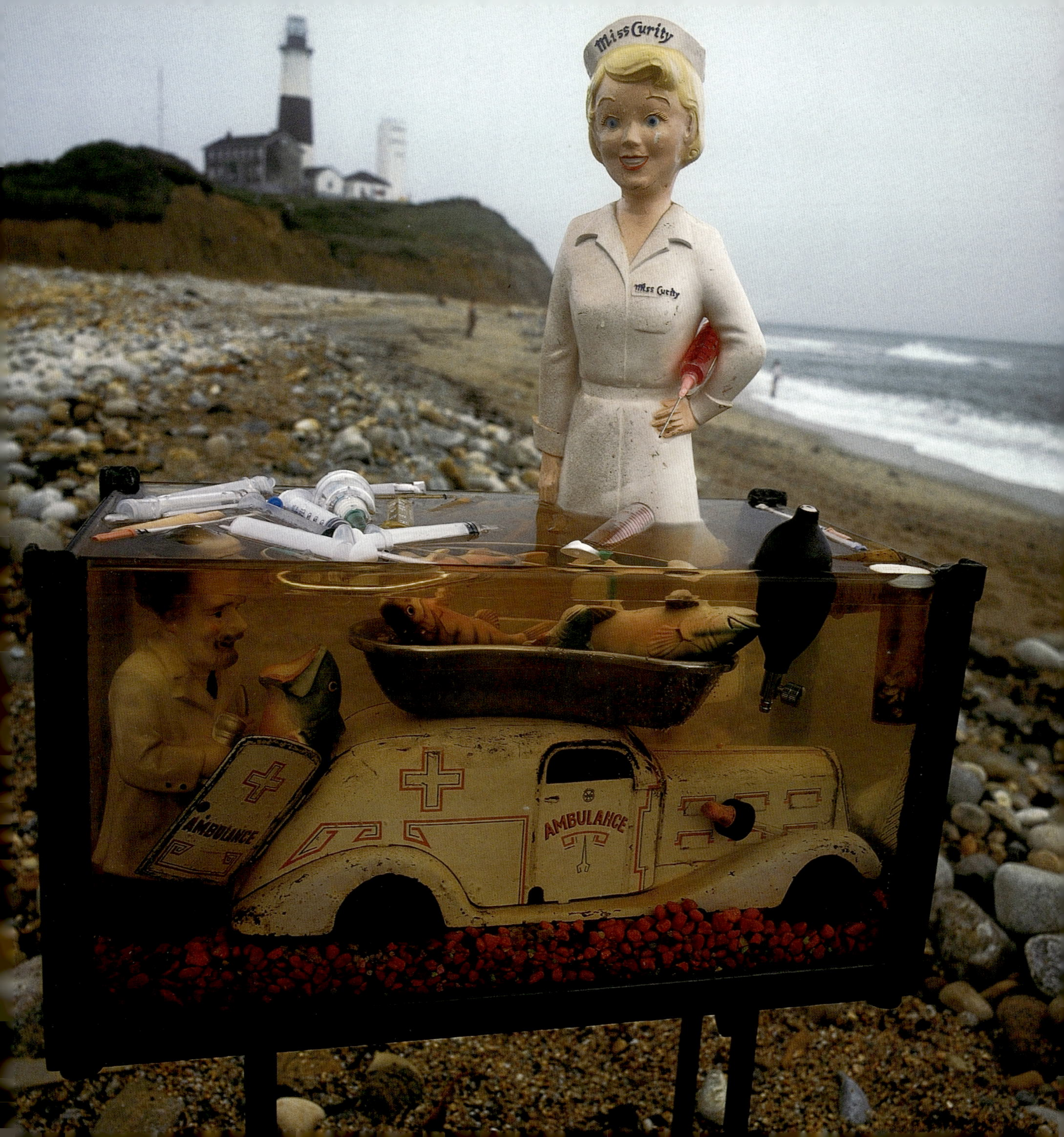

Miss Curity
Miss Curity
Miss Curity
AMBULANCE
AMBULANCE

Like sunken drums of waste
And the toxins they contain,
Even sun and rain
Could take the life they now sustain.

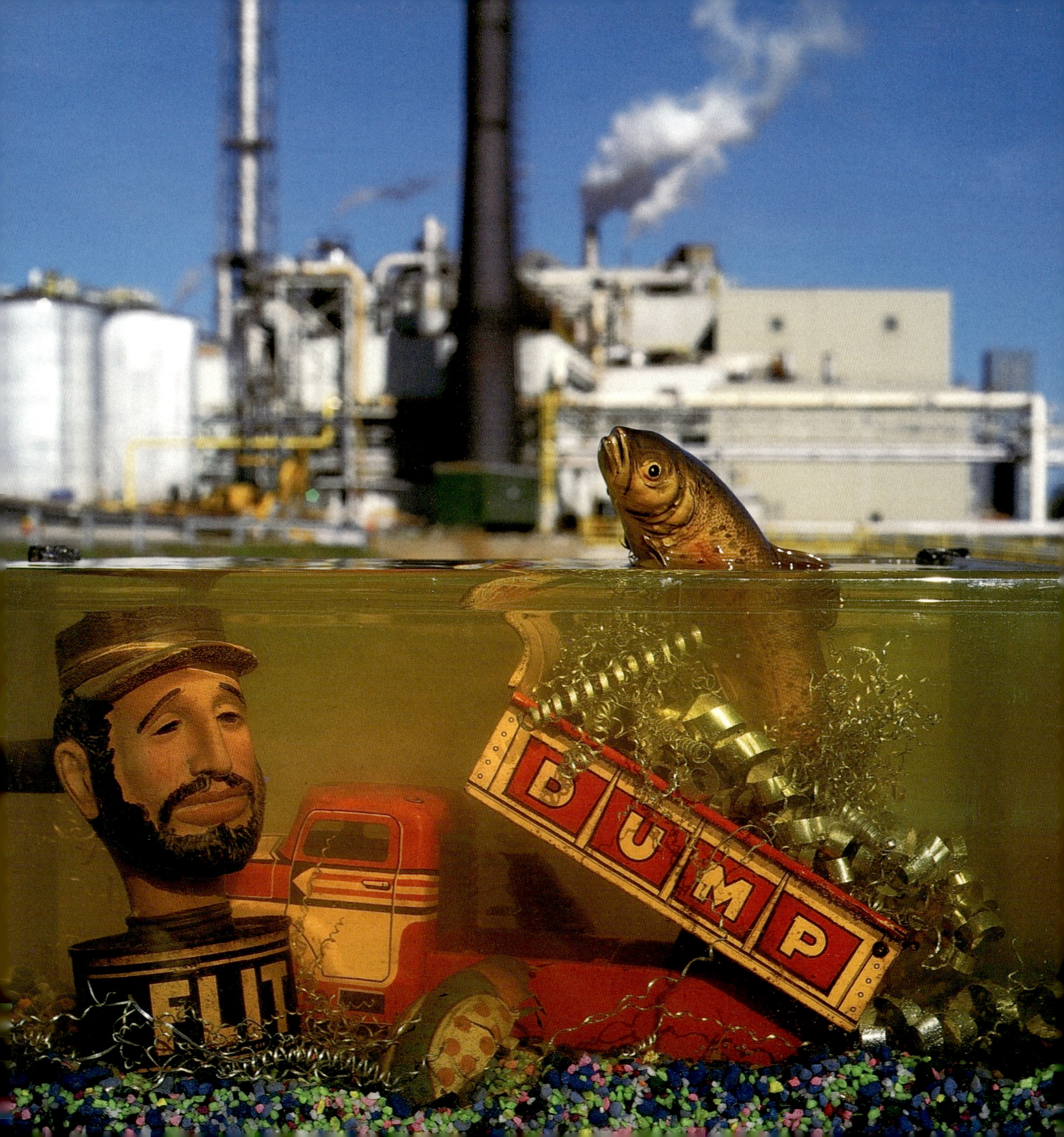

FLIT
DUMP

The fisherman saw that humankind
Would rapidly follow in decline
His marine and lacustrine
Water-breathing brethren.

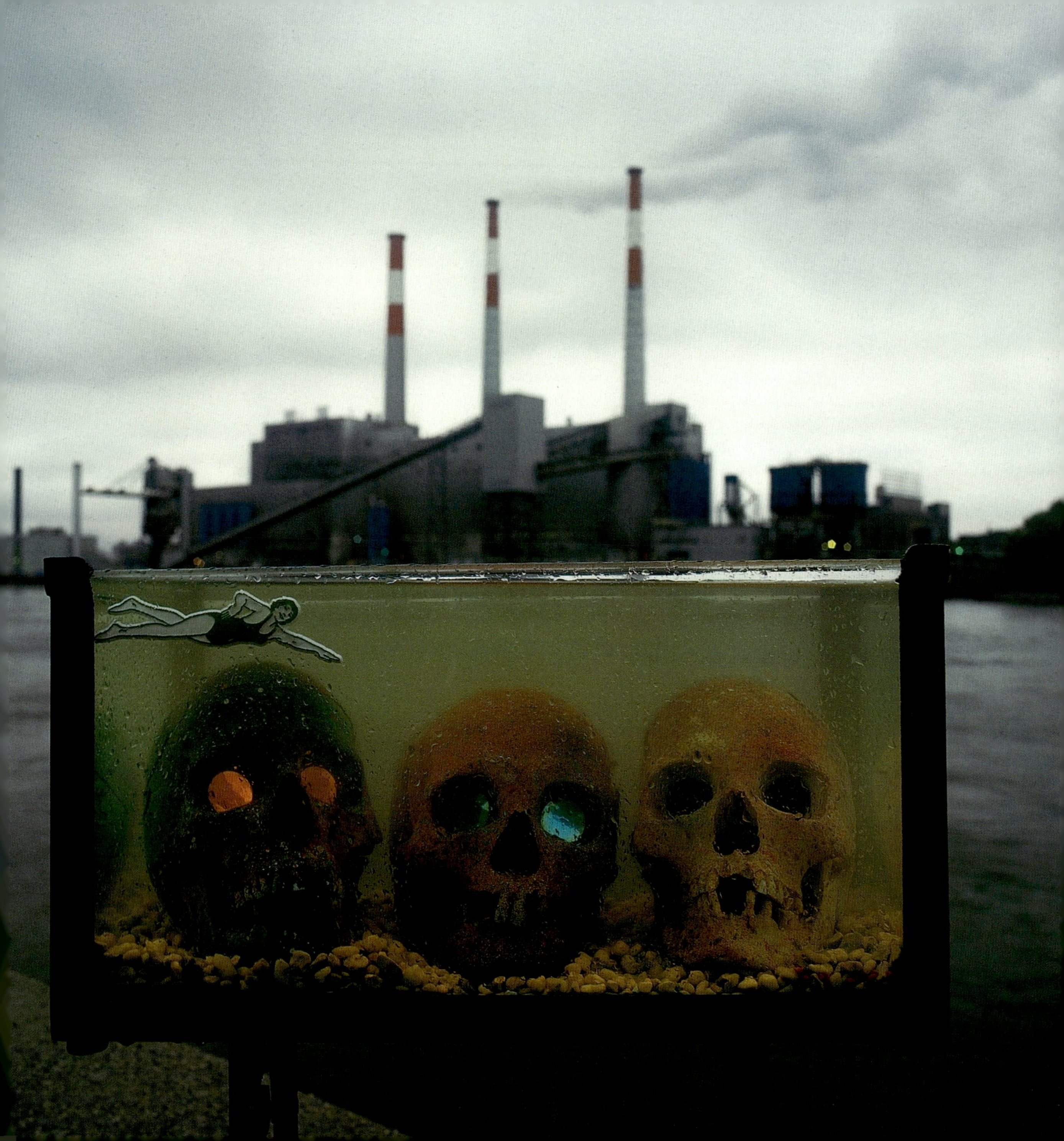

And thinking of what he must do
To repair the damage done,
He cast off his line and sailed
Homeward toward the setting sun.

132

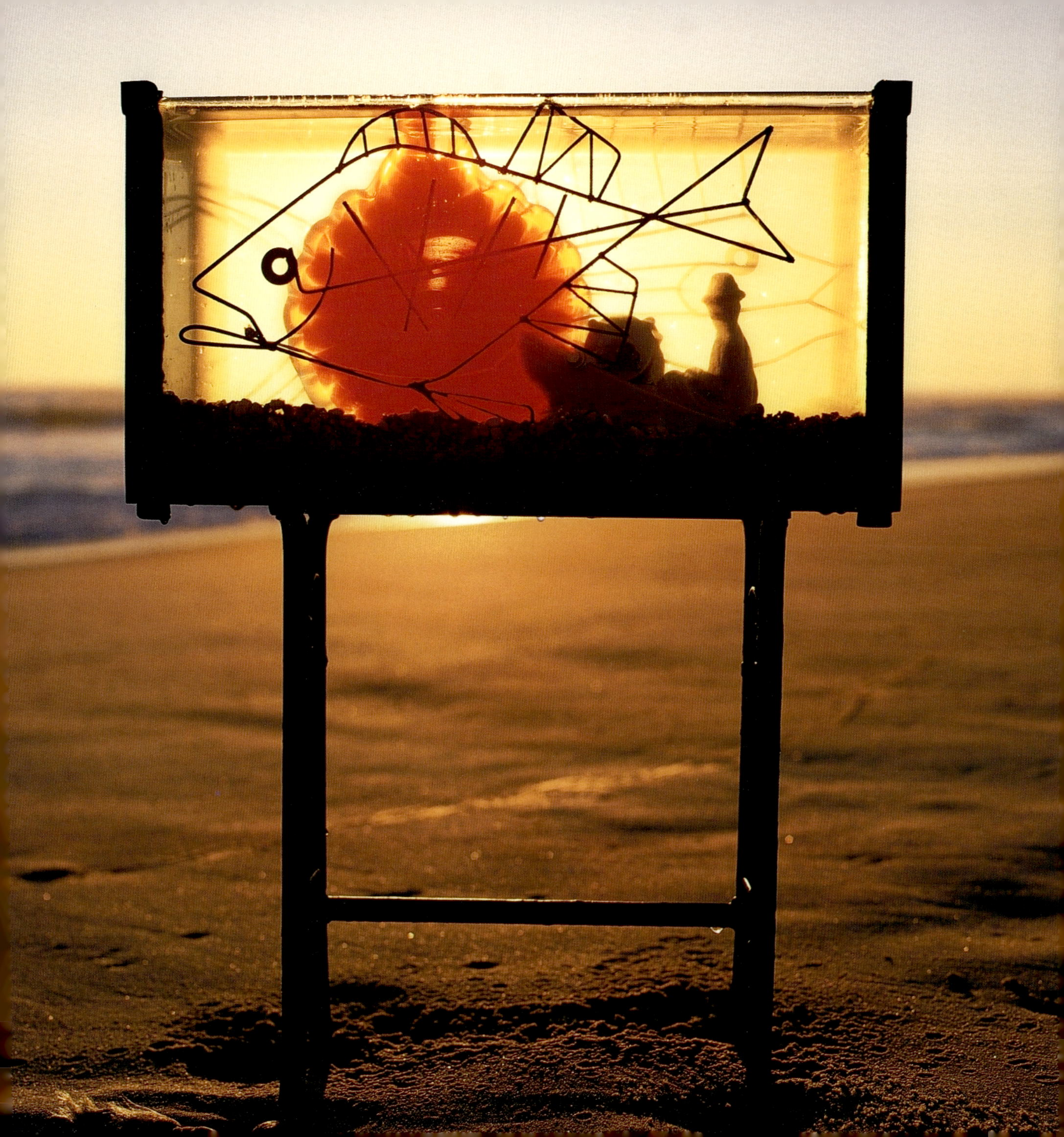

Men and fish are not alone
Living on this delicate blue sphere;
And with some luck and a little care,
Both will go on happily living here.

134]

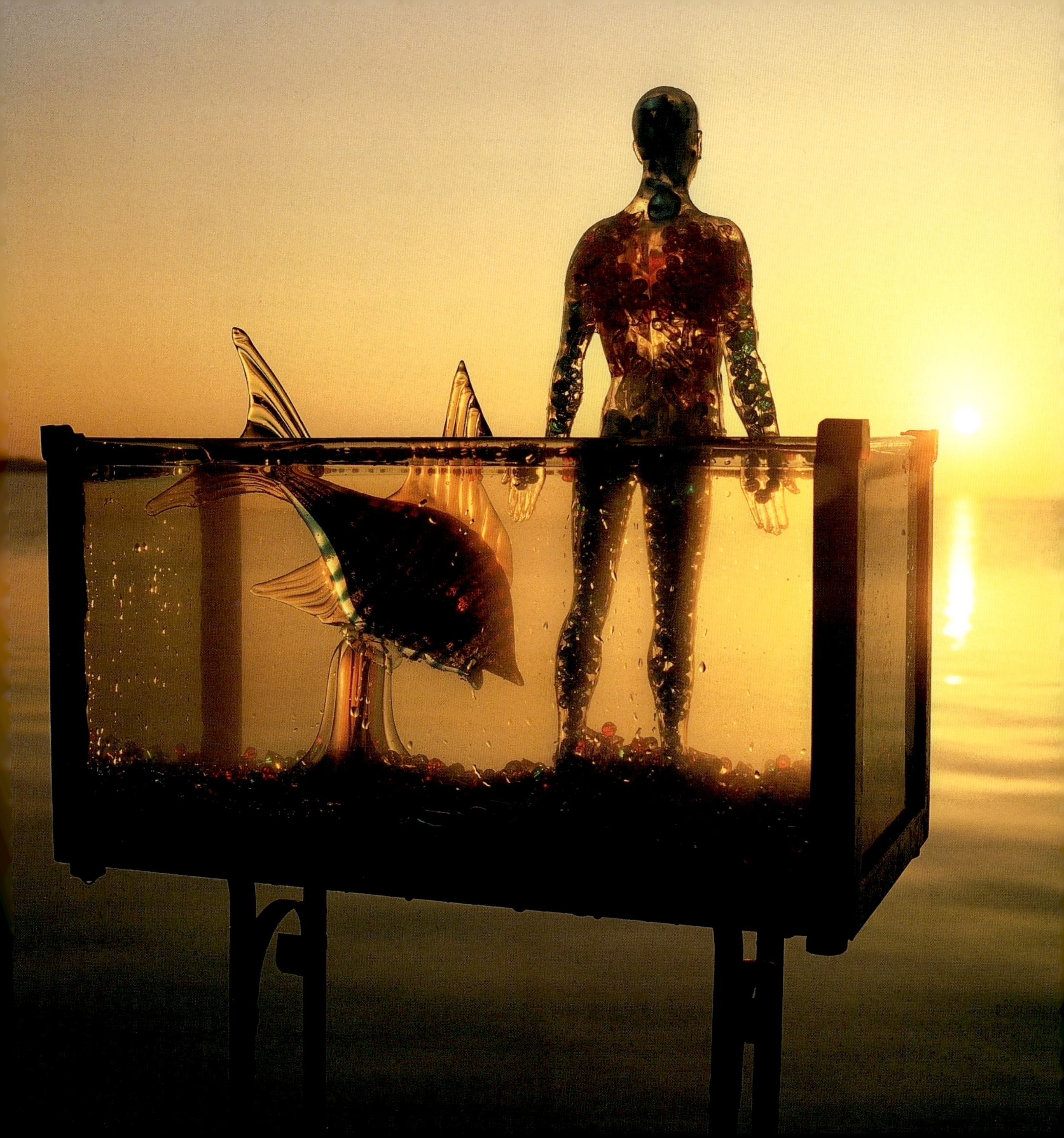

Afterword

"Il ne faut jamais parler sur le lac; ça pourrait effrayer les poissons."
(One must never talk when upon the lake; you will only scare the fish away.)
  —Alphonse Sénéchal, a French Canadian fisherman, to his son Pierre, age eight.

Like all my projects, *Fish Tank Sonata* seemed to begin rather accidentally one summer. I had rented a small cottage overlooking the Hudson River near Catskill, New York. The owner was a female photographer who, like myself, was a lover of flea markets and thrift shops. Her home was filled with "collectibles" from the forties and fifties, and I thought I might do some still lifes with them. But I didn't have a theme.

Catskill, coincidentally, had been the home of the famous Hudson River painter Thomas Cole, who in 1839 had begun a series of four paintings called *The Voyage of Life*. Rich with sentimental Victorian symbolism, they present the four stages of a man's life. The first depicts a small child in a tiny boat upon the "stream of life" emerging from the cave of the "mysterious past." The next image, *Youth...Full of Day Dreams,* imagines a "palace in the sky." Then the stormy scene titled *Manhood* indicates the "troubles and sorrows of middle age." In the last painting, *Old Age,* the white-bearded voyager, still in his boat but accompanied now by a guardian angel, gazes in rapture at "glimpses of immortal life."

Quite by chance, on one of the shelves in my cottage was a pink ceramic figure of a fisherman in a rowboat, and so I decided I would create an allegory similar to Coles's of the four stages of life.

But how, I wondered, was I to arrange the still life materials within the landscape? I knew I needed some sort of outdoor container, and it occurred to me to use an aquarium actually filled with water. But I soon discovered that the aquariums in pet shops were ugly, modern things trimmed in black plastic, and I feared that my project was collapsing. However, while driving through the mountains, I became lost and stumbled upon an old wooden mill by a waterfall. In the mill was an antique shop, and although there were no aquariums, the owner said that his mother had some in her attic. We drove to her house, and from her wheelchair she indicated that she would be happy to sell them. Upstairs in the gloomy attic I was thrilled to find a beautiful, hundred-year-old tank with beveled edges and a slate bottom. And so began *Fish Tank Sonata.*

I decided it would be not only the narrative of an angler's journey through space and time but also a partially auto-biographical narrative reflecting the process of how I had evolved into the photographer I am. The story would develop the parallel theme of how the snapshooter, like a hunter or fisherman, develops intuition, patience, and a delicate sense of timing in order to catch his elusive quarry on the fly. The sequence of images would detail the acquisition of vision, both through formal study with a master and from direct experience with the world. Each tableau would be a kind of visual parable—an emblematic installment, adding piece by piece to the fisherman's expanding education.

In certain tribal cultures animals, plants, and even inanimate objects are seen as gods come down, and they are considered to be visitors. These sojourning spirits take material form and make their fleshly bodies available as food to sustain human life. However, they must be treated as honored guests, and when they are sent back to the spirit realm, it must be done generously with thankful prayers and loving offerings. By doing these things, the spirits will be pleased with their passage amongst men and will return again to replenish the land and streams. If there is not this perpetual balance between giving and taking, the earth will become sterile, barren, and lifeless. It is this ancient reciprocal respect between man and creature that propels the natural engines of sustainable abundance. This is the message that the red snapper is trying to inculcate into the fisherman as he travels his watery course.

By broadening his narrowly focused obsession with "the catch of the day," the fisherman has expanded his band of reception and become attuned to the multichannel levels of his complex environment. By opening himself to this kind of two-way conversation, he not only succeeds but also survives in a self-renewing ecosystem. Fisherman, photographer, or mythic hero—we must all finally learn how to cast the line lightly and pulsate joyfully in unison with the singing, overlapping edges of the natural world.

Arthur Tress

List of Locations

The photographs in this book were shot in the following places:

Acknowledgments

I would like to thank the MacDowell Colony and Yaddo for their support in providing much-needed studio space. For their early support in creating exhibitions of *Fish Tank Sonata,* I would like to extend my gratitude to James Wyman of the Visual Studies Workshop in Rochester, New York; to Gloria Chalmers of the Portfolio Gallery, Edinburgh, Scotland; and to Trudy Wilner Stack of the Center for Creative Photography in Tuscon, Arizona. And in appreciation to my friends Roy Staab, Phillip Seymour, Sharon Cumberland, Nathan Farb, James Shields Jr., Michael Mastrangelo, and Tobin Keller, for help in scouting out props and locations. Also thanks to my editors, Garth Battista, John Wood, and Terry Hackford, for culling down an ocean of material and also to our designer, Michael Ian Kaye, for his striking amplification of my concept.

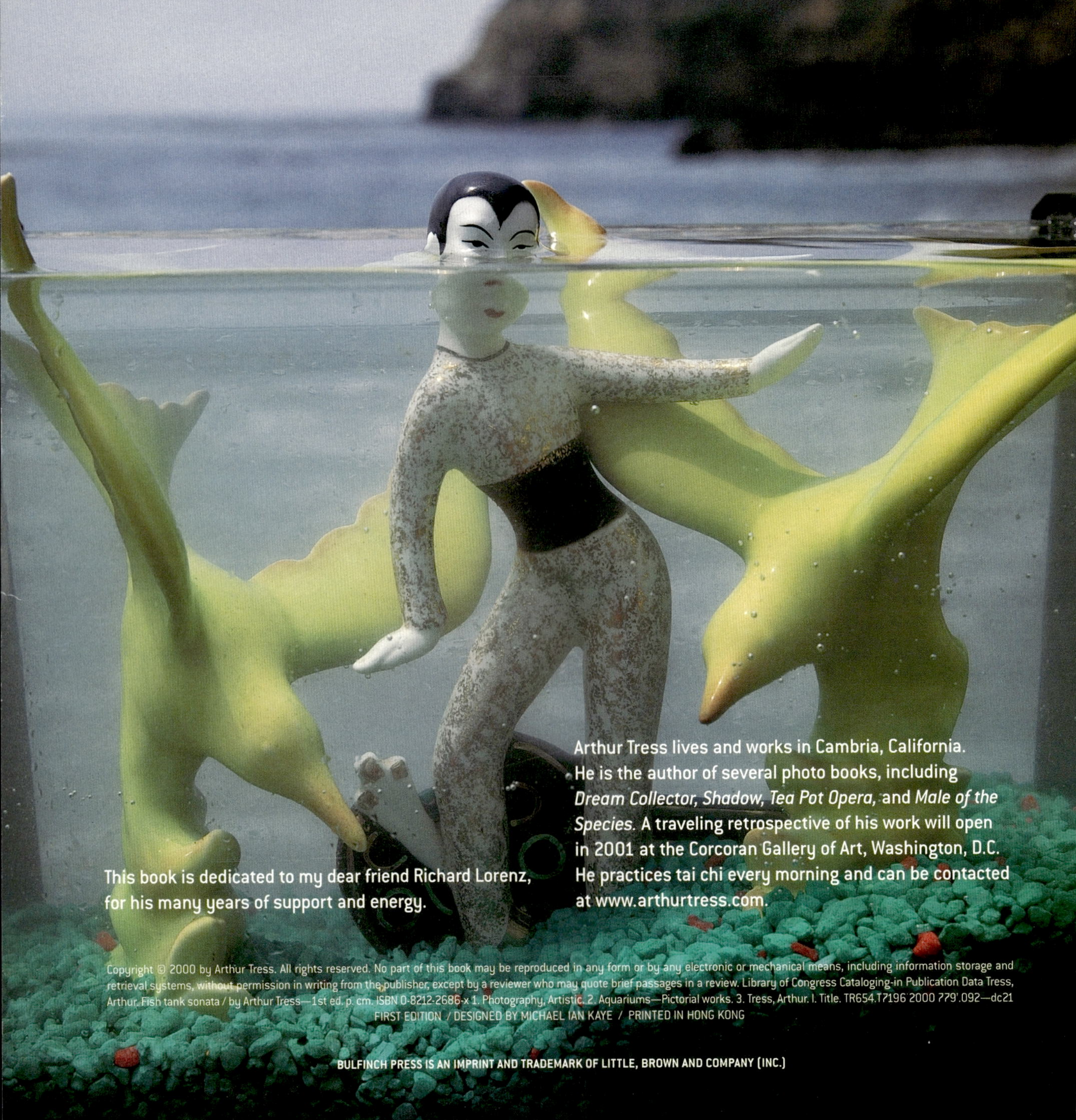
Arthur Tress lives and works in Cambria, California.
He is the author of several photo books, including
Dream Collector, Shadow, Tea Pot Opera, and Male of the
Species. A traveling retrospective of his work will open
in 2001 at the Corcoran Gallery of Art, Washington, D.C.
He practices tai chi every morning and can be contacted
at www.arthurtress.com.
This book is dedicated to my dear friend Richard Lorenz,
for his many years of support and energy.
Copyright © 2000 by Arthur Tress. All rights reserved. No part of this book may be reproduced in any form or by any electronic or mechanical means, including information storage and retrieval systems, without permission in writing from the publisher, except by a reviewer who may quote brief passages in a review. Library of Congress Cataloging-in Publication Data Tress, Arthur. Fish tank sonata / by Arthur Tress—1st ed. p. cm. ISBN 0-8212-2686-x 1. Photography, Artistic. 2. Aquariums—Pictorial works. 3. Tress, Arthur. I. Title. TR654.T7196 2000 779'.092—dc21
FIRST EDITION / DESIGNED BY MICHAEL IAN KAYE / PRINTED IN HONG KONG
BULFINCH PRESS IS AN IMPRINT AND TRADEMARK OF LITTLE, BROWN AND COMPANY (INC.)